77th Congress, 1st Session - - - - - House Document No. 13, pt. 1

ANNUAL REPORT OF THE
BOARD OF REGENTS OF
THE SMITHSONIAN INSTITUTION
1940

MASKED MEDICINE SOCIETIES of the IROQUOIS

by

W. N. Fenton

(Publication 3606)

UNITED STATES
GOVERNMENT PRINTING OFFICE
WASHINGTON : 1941

Reprint Series Editor – W. G. Spittal

Dr. Wm. N. Fenton

Harold Furlong photo, N.Y.S. Museum. Photo provided courtesy of W. N. Fenton.

MASKED MEDICINE SOCIETIES OF THE IROQUOIS

By WILLIAM N. FENTON
Bureau of American Ethnology

[With 25 plates]

INTRODUCTION

The Iroquois of New York and Ontario are among our oldest reservation Indians. Since the Revolution they have occupied diminishing areas within their ancient domain, and during the last century their settlements have been within marketing distance of large white trading centers that have become important eastern cities. It is a curious circumstance that Iroquois culture has not entirely disappeared in the face of our own civilization. Perhaps this is because it is only recently that the cities have grown and reached out to engulf the reservation communities. The older Indian people complain increasingly that the modern generation are failing to learn Indian languages or participate enthusiastically in tribal ceremonies. Nevertheless, within a day's journey from New York City there survive five conservative Iroquois communities in which, semiannually in spring and fall, the faithful leaders of the Society of Faces manage to muster enough ragged zealots to wear wooden masks and drive disease from their houses. The ethnologist may then, if he chooses, witness ancient ceremonies almost in his dooryard without going to the Southwest.

Longhouse groups.—The conservative Iroquois communities are located near the centers where Handsome Lake, the Seneca prophet, preached during the first 15 years of the nineteenth century, and on the reserves to which his disciples emigrated. These "real" or "longhouse people" live clustered about a dance house or ceremonial structure, called the longhouse, where they gather for social and religious purposes. The longhouse fires yet burn on the Onondaga Reservation near Syracuse (pl. 1, fig. 1) and on the three Seneca reservations neighboring Buffalo. The so-called Pagan Senecas kindle their fires at Tonawanda, at Coldspring on the Allegheny River, and at Newtown on Cattaraugus Reservation. Descendants of the Iroquois who moved west of the Niagara River into Canada at the close of the Revolution to settle along the banks of

3

the Grand River in Six Nations Reserve comprise four bands of Handsome Lake's adherents. The Upper Cayuga have their longhouse at Soursprings, Onondaga longhouse stands by Mackenzie Creek opposite Middleport (pl. 1, fig. 2), nearby is the third or Seneca longhouse with a congregation of mixed Onondaga, Cayuga, and Seneca descent, and the fourth longhouse is down below Peter Atkins' corners among the stronger band of Lower Cayuga. The Oneida near St. Thomas, farther west, have a longhouse, but neither among the Oneida, who early came under New England Christian influence, nor among the Catholic Mohawks of the St. Lawrence, who have recently been missionized from Onondaga, is there any great number of longhouse people.[1] As might be expected, the rituals of the masked shamanistic societies are best preserved in the more conservative centers of the Seneca and among the mixed Onondaga and Cayuga of Grand River.

Ethnological importance of collections.—Wooden masks from the Iroquois that are prominently displayed in eastern museums have considerable ethnological importance as well as popular appeal. Lewis H. Morgan seems to have been the first to collect Iroquois masks, and the literature on the so-called False-faces begins with his publication in 1851 of a line drawing of a mask, which he had acquired among the Onondaga of Canada, together with a terse statement of beliefs regarding the False-faces, the organization of the band, a reference to their preventing a cholera epidemic at Tonawanda in 1849, a description of their curing activities, and the depredations committed by small thieving boys disguised as False-faces at the Midwinter Festival.[2] Although J. V. H. Clark made somewhat earlier observations of the False-faces in the Onondaga Midwinter Festival of 1841,[3] the articles by DeCost Smith, the artist, are more reliable as source materials.[4] Smith drew the attention of the Reverend William M. Beauchamp to the function of the masks, which he had discovered in an Indian's attic, and to the problem of their antiquity among the Iroquois.[5] Besides his articles, Smith executed a series of animated illustrations which he deposited with his mask

---

[1] For a map and summary of populations of reservations and settlements of modern Iroquoian peoples see the author's recent paper, Problems arising from the historic northeastern position of the Iroquois. Smithsonian Misc. Coll., vol. 100, pp. 214–215, 1940.

[2] Morgan, L. H., League of the . . . Iroquois, vol. 1, pp. 157–160, 204–205, New York, 1901.

[3] Clark, Joshua V. H., Onondaga; or reminiscences of earlier and later times, vol. 1, p. 57, Syracuse, N. Y., 1849.

[4] Smith, DeCost, Witchcraft and demonism of the modern Iroquois. Journ. Amer. Folklore, vol. 1, pp. 184–194, 1888; Additional notes on Onondaga witchcraft and Ho ⁿ-do'-i. Ibid., vol. 2, pp. 277–281, 1889.

[5] Beauchamp, William M., Aboriginal uses of wood in New York. New York State Mus. Bull. 89, p. 187, 1905.

collections in several museums.⁶ Somewhat later David Boyle, of Toronto, was stimulated to make similar observations of the False-face ceremonies among the Iroquois of Grand River and to publish brief notices of his collecting activities.⁷ His collections now repose in the Royal Ontario Museum of Archaeology in Toronto along with the Chiefswood Collection of Pauline Johnson, the Mohawk poetess.

Several large study collections resulted from the activities of Harriet Maxwell Converse, a poet and journalist, who during the years 1881 to 1903 was an enthusiastic collector of Seneca Iroquois materials. Her success was partly due to adoption by the Senecas and later by the Onondagas, who installed her as an honorary chief of the Six Nations.⁸ There are over 100 Converse masks in the New York State Museum (in Albany), and others in the Peabody Museum of Harvard University and in the American Museum of Natural History (New York); and Joseph Keppler, her successor among the Seneca, has deposited his mask collections in the Museum of the American Indian. However, Converse's brief published utterances on masks (1899 and 1908) and the accession records which sometimes accompany her collections make one suspicious of her field work. There are poetic titles for the masks, suggesting fanciful roles, such as "war and scalp, clan, maternity, bird, pipe-smoker's, sun-rise, dead chief, etc.," that no field worker among the Iroquois since her time has substantiated.

M. R. Harrington,⁹ who visited the Canadian Iroquois in the summer of 1907, turned over to the American Museum gratifyingly full accession records which suggest only a few rather general mask types that agree with the findings of Morgan, Smith, Parker, and the writer. Even Parker himself, who had access to Mrs. Converse's notes and to some of her informants, found only four classes of masks based on function.¹⁰ We conclude, therefore, that Mrs. Converse wrote into the records more than she was told, or that she posed leading questions to willing informants who politely assented.

---

⁶ The Onondaga Historical Society of Syracuse has the masks that Smith presented to Beauchamp, but the American Museum of Natural History has the masks that he published and his drawings. Following his recent death, his remaining collections were divided between the latter institution and the Museum of the Amercan Indian, Heye Foundation.

⁷ Boyle, David, Society of the False Faces, Ontario Arch. Rep. 1898, pp. 157-160, 1898; and Iroquois medicine man's Mask. Ibid., 1899, pp. 27-29, 1900.

⁸ Converse, H. M., and Parker, Arthur C., ed., Myths and legends of the New York State Iroquois. New York State Mus. Bull. 125, pp. 17-29, 1908.

⁹ Harrington, M. R., Some unusual Iroquois specimens. Amer. Anthrop., n. s., vol. 11, No. 1, pp. 85-91, 1909.

¹⁰ Parker, A. C., Secret medicine societies of the Seneca. Amer. Anthrop., n. s., vol. 2, No. 2, p. 179, 1909.

The False-faces raise some problems of theoretical importance. We may, as Goldenweiser suggested,[11] consider the wood-carving process from the standpoint of technique and artistic styles; or we may consider the organization of the Society of Faces (the False-face Company) and its relation to other medicine fraternities and show how their function is in turn patterned by the concept of reciprocal services between the dual division of Iroquois society. Thus every ceremony is conceived as being given by one half of the tribe for its cousins, the opposite half.

Finally, when we speak of masks, we must always remember, as Hewitt[12] stoutly insisted, that the "Faces" are really "likenesses," in the sense that they are portraits of mythological beings, and they are not masks for the purpose of concealment. The mask itself is only a symbol which operates on the principle of substituting a part for the whole, and the wearer behaves as if he were the supernatural being whom he impersonates. These supernaturals are Wind or Disease Gods of two classes and several varieties, and they are portrayed by wooden or husk faces that are described in the myths, but their human counterparts show a great deal of individual variation.

The need of an adequate study.—Our extensive collections of Iroquois masks are frequently undocumented or labelled so as to conform to rather dubious sources and in direct contradiction to the concepts which the Iroquois themselves hold regarding the masks and their function. Instead of catalog entries, the masks are attended with a lore that has come down through successive curators as to their supposed function. It is therefore not strange that the functions which have been ascribed to the masks on the basis of their appearance and the classification that has grown up in the museum differ from the ideas entertained by the Iroquois who still use them. At some time in the past two streams of culture have diverged, and I feel that the Iroquois have been the less speculative and therefore the more trustworthy custodians of tradition. That such confusion exists in the face of a rather extensive literature on

---

[11] Prof. A .A. Goldenweiser and F. W. Waugh studied the Iroquois at Grand River for the National Museum of Canada following 1912. Masks interested both men: their role in society and the development of artistic styles intrigued Goldenweiser, the sociologist; while for Waugh, masks were part of material culture. Both men joined forces to record the carving process. Goldenweiser, A. A., On Iroquois Work, 1912. Summ. Rep. Geol. Surv. Canada for the calendar year 1912, pp. 474–475.

[12] J. N. B. Hewitt during many years of field work was interested in the problem of the "Faces." His informants, Chiefs John A. Gibson, Joshua and John Buck, Jr., were the best available among the Iroquois of Grand River. Neither his publications (Seneca fiction . . . (with Jeremiah Curtain), 32d Ann. Rep. Bur. Amer. Ethnol., pp. 61, 67, 1918; Iroquoian cosmology, pt. 2, 43d Rep. Bur. Amer. Ethnol., pp. 533, 610, 1928; The culture of the Indians of eastern Canada, Expl. and Field-work Smithsonian Inst. in 1928, p. 182, 1929; and ibid., 1929, p. 201, 1930) nor his manuscripts on the Faces provide the least support for Mrs. Converse's imaginative titles.

the so-called False-faces only serves to emphasize the need of an adequate monograph. Such a study would require a description and classification of masks in terms of the myths in which they figure and in terms of the rituals in which they participate. It would be interesting to know whether this classification agrees with a typological classification based on the masks themselves. It is important to know how individuals join the Society of Faces. How is the Society organized internally, and how is it related to other Iroquois medicine societies? This requires a detailed account of the rituals and a study of its ceremonial equipment and procedure. Finally an estimate is needed of the importance of masked shamanism in Iroquois life, and of its position in the ethnographic perspective of the Northeast.

Some years ago while engaged in field work among the Seneca I approached these problems in a general paper.[13] Its publication elicited rather unexpected responses representing a wide range of reading interests outside of ethnology, and it soon went out of print. Masks evidently hold an especial fascination for dramatists, sculptors, and decorators, and a great variety of hobbyists; while shamanism has implications for medicine and all those professions that hem in the periphery of the human psyche.[14]

Purpose.—The present paper attempts several things. First, it revises the original statement in an effort to clarify the unsolved problems that hung over from the first paper. Second, it includes new information from further field work among other Iroquoian groups and from the study of museum collections that were not available to me in 1935. Finally, it republishes the original materials together with the results of recent studies and makes them available to a wider public.

Problems.—The problems that confront us in the present study are essentially those of the relationship of mental stereotypes and overt behavior. First, what are the formal types of masks and how do the Iroquois classify them? To what extent do the mask types reflect cultural stereotypes given in mythology; and, conversely, to what extent are the formal character of spirits in the myths, and the shapes they assume in dreams and visions, projections into the spirit-

---

[13] Fenton, Wm. N., The Seneca Society of Faces. Sci. Monthly, vol. 44, pp. 215–238, March 1937.

[14] A number of general papers on masks and shamanistic societies have appeared. The relation of "Masks and moieties as a culture complex" has been considered by A. L. Kroeber and C. Holt (Journ. Roy. Anthrop. Inst. Great Britain and Ireland, n. s., vol. 50, pp. 452–460, 1920). Clark Wissler has made good use of the Iroquois material in a general paper on masks (The lore of the Demon Mask. Nat. Hist., vol. 28, No. 4, pp. 339–352, 1928), and Kenneth Macgowan and Herman Rosse (Masks and demons. Harcourt, Brace & Co., 1923) have discussed the relations of masks to the theater, reflecting the rather wide interest in the subject outside of anthropology.

world of the grotesque wooden masks worn by human beings?[15] If there are local styles of carving, we must consider how the individual learns to carve and the opportunities for the free play of his whims in devising new forms. There is always the problem of disregard of native theory in ritual practice. Thus, if there are formal distinctions between mask types, based on myths, the members of the society may not consistently use the same mask always to portray the same being, or to perform a consistent function in a ceremony. The history of masked shamanism among the Iroquois may help explain the relationship of the Society of Faces to the other medicine societies, the orders of membership, and the form and content of the masked rituals.

Method.—This study was first of all an attempt to find out the meaning and uses of masks in museum collections. I went to the Seneca at Allegany in 1933 with a series of photographs of masks that had been collected among them. Informants expressed great interest in pictures of their handiwork and they identified various masks as belonging to individuals who employed them in certain ceremonies, and I recorded these comments togethed with the Seneca names for various mask types. This procedure led to a number of myths and folk tales involving the masks, which I took down. The method was not standardized or controlled, but it was repeated with several informants who checked each other.

Direct information was solicited of all informants on origin myths and their personal histories as members of the Society of Faces. Case histories of members disclosed information on illnesses, membership through dreams and visions, hysteria, and accounts of participation in cures, as well as lengthy descriptions of the rituals.

Actual rituals of the masked societies were observed during field trips to the Seneca of Allegany and Tonawanda, and to the Onondaga outside Syracuse, N. Y.;[16] while only descriptions of the Cattaraugus Seneca and Canadian Iroquois masked ceremonies were obtained. However, observation provides only background for questioning because one observes both significant and accidental detail, and not until an informant describes the same performance does the ethnologist appreciate what the ceremony actually means to participants. Otherwise, the observer makes a complete but spurious record of behavior, and he fails to grasp what is culturally meaningful. A motion pic-

---

[15] Goldenweiser, A. A., Early civilization . . . pp. 231–232, New York, 1922.
[16] Field work among the Seneca at Allegany from June to September 1933, and January–February and July and August 1934, was conducted for the Institute of Human Relations at Yale University. Two and one-half years at Tonawanda for the U. S. Indian Service afforded ample opportunity to witness the masked ceremonies. Recently, two seasons of field work among the Seneca of New York and among the Cayuga-Onondaga of Six Nations, Ontario, for the Bureau of American Ethnology have yielded much additional information.

ture record of the ceremonies would have the same weakness. Only during the last season have I been permitted to photograph the False-face ceremonies, but here again it has been more successful to have selected informants compose a series of what they consider the essential phases of a curing ritual. While the camera freezes characteristic posture and gesture, it also catches the contemporary scene. For this reason I had a young Seneca artist, Ernest Smith, of Tonawanda, make some illustrations of the False-face ceremonies, as he imagined they might have been performed a century earlier. At the same time he was executing an extensive series for the Rochester Museum of Arts and Sciences and his work entailed consultation with my older informants. Smith's illustrations, therefore, are to the photographs as informant descriptions are to the ethnologist's observations. They stand in the relationship of ideal patterns, cultural concepts, to actual practice.

Observation coupled with photography is particularly rewarding in studies of material culture. In this way I recorded the technique of mask making at Tonawanda, Coldspring, and Grand River, noting positions of work and ways of handling tools. Out of this emerged the best material on artistic styles, the role of the individual in devising new forms, education in handicrafts, and the tyranny of local canons of art. The whole mask-making process, which was formerly ritualized, is still hedged in by the fragments of a broken-down ceremonial procedure.

Because up to 1937 my data on mask types contained nothing comparable to the poetic titles that Converse had given to her masks, it seemed advisable to study her extensive collections in Albany and New York. I employed the technique of recording on slips information on a selected series of criteria that increased or narrowed as the study progressed, such as color, form of chin, mouth, nose, presence or absence of supplementary wrinkles and superorbital ridges, spines on nose bridge, shape and method of attaching tin eyes, presence of tobacco bags; and on the back: number of holes for head and hair attachment, indications of use, carving methods, species of wood, and other noteworthy features. Then each specimen was photographed with the aid of a copy stand, and negatives were cataloged serially to agree with data sheets and the museum catalog. Over 100 masks were examined at the New York State Museum, 6 at the Montgomery County Historical Society, Fort Johnson, N. Y., 24 at the Royal Ontario Museum of Archaeology, Toronto, and 16 of the older masks in the Rochester Museum of Arts and Sciences. Only 35, a small part of the extensive collections of the Museum of the American Indian, were examined at the Annex during 1 day, and photographs have been obtained subsequently of specimens on permanent exhibit which it was not advisable to disturb. Other photographs have been generously supplied by Dr. W. C. McKern, of the Milwaukee Public Museum, the Peabody Museum at Harvard University, which I was unable to visit, and the United States National Museum, the National Museum of Canada, and the American Museum of Natural History.

In using photographs for sampling the knowledge of informants, I did not succeed in devising a controlled technique for testing and recording their attitudes toward the pictures. All informants regarded pictures of masks with great interest, and frequently with considerable amusement which they often shared with passing Indians; and the amount often varied with the horrific appearance of the mask and its supposed power, or sometimes as it furnished an excellent caricature of some local personality.[17] The Iroquois are both amused and awed by these pathetically humorous portraits of supernatural disease beings who so dominate their dream life. Nevertheless, if we did not obtain from all informants a consistent appraisal of mask types, very often an informant would recognize the picture as of a mask that he had made or one that he had seen in some ceremony, and all these incidents provided grist for our mill.

The pictures should prove of further value in segregating formal mask types and art styles by localities. It is possible to analyze the masks and plot the distribution of characteristic features, such as mouth shape, bent nose, spines on forehead, and presence of supplementary wrinkles. This is one way of establishing local and tribal styles. We compare these with concepts of informants and discover that much of formal art exists on the level of unconscious behavior patterns.

The practice of recording extensive texts in the native language of myths, prayers, and even accounts of individual participation in culture, has become a bit unfashionable of late in ethnology. This is partly because the texts often became an end in themselves, or they remained unpublished because the authors were not satisfied that they were accurately translated, or they reached such proportions that the translation became an impracticable ordeal, and the recorders passed away before the end was achieved. Nevertheless, in the study of ceremonies there is no substitute for texts in the native language. Very often the prayer texts contain archaic words that are the keys to unlock concepts that are not verbalized by contemporary members of society. Therefore, apart from any interest in linguistic research, I early discovered that I had to record texts to get at the ethnological materials which I was seeking. Thus from our texts we derive a name for the "sponsor" of medicine society ceremonies which we recog-

---

[17] Miss Marjorie Lismer, who was cooperating in the same study, encountered similar reactions.

nize in a similar form in the writings of the seventeenth century Jesuit missionaries, and from this we infer that the present role of "sponsor" has a historical depth of 300 years and that it is probably aboriginal. This helps to explain why the business of feast-making permeates all of Iroquois ceremonialism.[18]

Finally, to place the complex of Iroquois masked shamanism in ethnographic perspective the comparative method might be employed. If we can show that the complex has a historical depth reaching back to the first white contacts with the Iroquois, it would be relevant to investigate whether the Iroquois possess the complex in a greater degree of detail than their Algonquian neighbors. If we could determine the center whence masking spread throughout the northeast, some light might shine on the problem of whether Iroquois masking is a diagnostic trait pointing to their alleged southern origin, or whether it is related to northern shamanism and the use of masks across the Arctic littoral, or whether the complex was original with the Iroquois themselves from whom it spread to the neighboring Delaware. However, it is beyond the scope of this present paper to do more than stake out this problem.

MASK TYPES

The wooden masks or False-faces.—A few museum visitors may appreciate that the weird human likenesses which mock them from the showcases are actually memorials to generations of nightmares. They are wooden portraits of several types of mythical beings whom the Iroquois say only a little while ago inhabited the far rocky regions at the rim of the earth or wandered about in the forests. The Seneca term for mask is "Face" (gagǫ́hsa'); but the Onondaga more often call him "Hunchback" (hadu' 'i', or hǫdo· 'wi'(;[19] while the Mohawk are satisfied to use the term "Face" (gagu· 'wara(; and so they are called "False-faces" in the literature, and in "reservation English." Iroquois hunters, when traveling, frequently met strange, quasihuman beings who darted from tree to tree in the forests and who frequently appeared to be disembodied heads with long, snapping hair. They agreed not to molest human beings, saying that they merely wanted Indian tobacco (*Nicotiana rustica* L.) and mush to be made from the white corn meal which hunters and warriors carried. However, the being with the wry mouth and broken nose, whom the Seneca call "Great defender" (sʻagodyowe'hgo·waʻ), "The great humpbacked one" (hadu'i' go· 'naʻ) of the Onondaga, has appeared to few human

---

[18] For an elaboration of this method, see Sapir, E., Time perspective in aboriginal American culture . . . Canada Geol. Sur., Mem. 90, Anthrop. Ser. No. 13, p. 51 ff., Ottawa, 1916.

[19] *Phonetic note.*—The orthography employed in this paper has the same phonetic values as explained in Iroquois Suicide, Bur. Amer. Ethnol. Bull. 128, No. 14, 1941.

beings because he promised the Creator to abide in inaccesible places on the rim of the earth; but he is well known in mythology and by his human counterparts, the maskers that represent him in the ceremonies.

The Faces of the forest also claimed to possess the power to control sickness. They instructed the dreamers to carve likenesses in the form of masks, saying that whenever anyone makes ready the feast, invokes their help while burning Indian tobacco and sings the curing songs, supernatural power to cure disease will be conferred on human beings who wear the masks. The dancers should carry turtle rattles and speak a weird, unintelligible nasal language. They can scoop up glowing embers in their bare hands, without suffering burns when they blow hot ashes on the sick person. The masks are as varied as the visions and the artistic whims of the individual craftsmen who have carved them from single blocks of living basswood.

Native classification confused.—Natives themselves are confused when asked to classify False-faces. One old Seneca informant, Henry Redeye, told me there are as many False-face types as there are different people. Some are portraits of youths; others are of old men who have long, white hair and wrinkled faces. There are angry individuals with broken noses and mouths skewed to one side as if they had suffered paralytic strokes, who are apt to sweat and cause an owner illness if he neglects to supplicate them with tobacco offerings. Some have distended, open lips as if they were blowing ashes; a few with standing hair and raised eyebrows are whistling and merely want tobacco, while others protrude red tongues in pain, or laugh, revealing irregular rows of wooden or bone teeth. Their similarities are only those which the local culture has prescribed in dreams.

Tradition has dictated the forms which the faces assume in visions, and the features which the craftsmen emphasize when carving, the very features which the Indians mention when describing the original forest folk. It is sufficient for the carver to single out particular features of the face for artistic expression; the face portrays the being, and the wearer must dramatize his other attributes: his erect or slouching gait, his awful mien and the nonsensical, nasal speech which he accompanies by shaking a rattle. To the Indians, the total effect is both terrifying and extremely humorous.

Iroquois conceptions of the supernaturals whom these dramatizations represent have unquestionably been influenced by projecting in dreams the form of the masks and the behavior of the actors who appear in the ceremonies. Thus, as Goldenweiser pointed out:[20]

Various grotesque spirits must be regarded as derived either from dreams or visions or to be the outgrowth of the free play of the imagination. Not infrequently, artificial objects or artistic conventions must have had an influence

[20] Goldenweiser, A. A., Early civilization, pp. 231–232. New York, 1922.

on the formal character of spirits. Thus, it is highly probable that the False-face spirits of the Iroquois are the projections into the spiritual world of the grotesque wooden masks worn by the members of the False-face Society, . . .

Mask types depend on the use to which they are put. They are not rigidly definable on the basis of form alone because to a large extent use determines type. This is the old argument of form vs. function, of native theory and native practice which flies in the face of all over nice taxonomic distinctions based on form alone. Aside from the fact that a carver may be guided by the mythological incident of hadú'i' breaking his nose on the mountain and intend his mask as a representation of that being, a subsequent owner may disregard this in using the mask. Conversely, a mask which was never intended to represent more than a common face of the forest may in time perform the curing role of the great world-rim dweller in the doorkeeper ritual. Thus all the old masks do become ultimately "doctor" masks. And, occasionally, even some of the more potent "doctor" masks get into the hands of small boys who impersonate the beggars of the forest at the Midwinter Festival. Therefore, only within certain limits and allowing for such exceptions will an informant even attempt to assign a series of masks to specific functions and categories.

The dramatic behavior of the wearers of the masks counts more in the roles in which the masks appear than the form of the mask itself. Here individual talent in acting and dancing constitutes much of the effectiveness of ceremony. Certain individuals in every Iroquois community are known to be good prospects for the role of doorkeeper. Sometimes a good actor possesses a fine old mask that is suited to the role, and in time both he and his mask come to be associated with this role. But as he grows older he may be selected as conductor and he easily finds a younger man to wear his mask, but the community ordinarily has little difficulty in distinguishing the mask and its owner and in identifying the new actor.

In general, the masks have deep-set eyes, rendered bright by metal sconces, and large, frequently bent noses. The arched brows are deeply wrinkled and sometimes divided above the nose by a longitudinal crease or a comb of spines, which only one Seneca calls "Turtletail," because they resemble the processes on a mud turtle's tail. The mouth is the most variable feature, and runs through a whole range of contortions depending on mood, function, or locality. Both mouth corners may be upturned in a smile, or a grimace showing teeth; or the mouth is distended ovally for blowing ashes, sometimes with protruding tongue; or it is puckered as if whistling, or puckered with conventionalized tongue and spoonlike lips, which may be again bifunnelate for blowing ashes, or once more revealing teeth; then others have large, straight, distended lips, which may be twisted up at one corner to accompany a bent nose, or down at the other corner; and finally, both corners may turn down in an expression of utmost anguish. Thick, distended lips protrude beneath the nose, and a series of modifying wrinkles augment the distorted expression. Cheek bones are sometimes suggested, and a prominent chin, common on masks from Grand River, serves as a convenient grip for the wearer to adjust the mask to his face. The face is framed by a long wig, usually cut from black horsetails which fall on either side from a part in the middle of the forehead; but anciently, corn-husk braids, shredded basswood bast, or buffalo mane served as hair. Masks are commonly painted red or black.

Classification based on specimens.—In classifying the masks we must take into consideration formal types based on variations in the masks themselves and local styles of carving. Thus a particular formal feature, such as the bent nose or the twisted mouth, is apt to be shared among two or more local groups and tribes, but what distinguishes the masks of one local group, say the Senecas of Newtown, from the masks of artisans in another community, possibly the Onondagas of Grand River, is the manner with which the individual carver expresses his local artistic tradition in the general conformation of the whole face. Since the mouth is the mask's most variable feature, permitting us to range our photographs in a series of categories illustrating progressive changes from up-turned corners to down-turned corners, it seems a likely basis for distinguishing formal types. What gives this arrangement significance is the tendency of the Iroquois themselves to designate the mouth as a criterion for naming the masks. The masks, unlike individuals, do not have personal names except as they are given the names of the spirits who are their tutelaries. The names are rather descriptive referents to various facial expressions.

Thus one afternoon two Seneca informants, James Crow, of Newtown, and Chauncey Johnny John, of Coldspring, distinguished the following mouth types, while examining photographs of museum specimens. Naturally, they commenced with types most familiar to them in their own localities; and I append the remarks of other informants, Jesse Cornplanter, of Tonawanda, and Simeon Gibson (Onondaga-Cayuga), of Grand River, and Sherman Redeye, of Coldspring, where they seem pertinent. We begin at the middle of the series.

1. The crooked-mouth masks, a type so named because "his mouth is twisted" (ha'sagai·'de'), are commonest among all the Iroquois. One corner of the mouth is pulled down, or up. They occur among Seneca, Cayuga, and Onondaga of New York and Grand River. In the latter place carvers make them intentionally horrific to frighten away disease, and masks with bent noses and twisted mouths aug-

mented by many supplementary wrinkles constitute a local style (pl. 2, fig. 2).

2. The mask with straight lips, a type so named because "his mouth is straight" (hodesado'gɛ'dǫ), has straight distended lips like a duck bill across the whole face. This one, with its variants, together with the two that follow, is frequently ornamented with a crest of spines or "teeth" extending up the forehead from the nose bridge, but its symbolism is not clear (pl. 3, fig. 1).

3. The spoon-lipped or spoon-mouthed mask, with "double spoons made on it" (odo'gwa'sǫdǫ'), is the most easily recognized type. It consists of conventionalized flared lips or puckered lips as in blowing and a rudimentary tongue which projects beneath the pursed mouth aperture (pl. 3, fig. 2). Spoon-lipped masks are rare among the Iroquois of Grand River but are common at Newtown on Cattaraugus Seneca Reservation, and they have been in use since the earliest memory of my informants. The Newtown Senecas consider the straight-lipped and the spoon-lipped masks, which they pair in the doorkeeper ritual, to be classic Seneca representations of the great supernatural world-rim dweller. However, the spoon lips take the form of two funnels among the Seneca of Coldspring on Allegheny River.

4. The hanging-mouth mask is so named because "the corners of his mouth are hanging" (hosɛ' 'dǫ'), not unlike the muse of tragedy (pl. 4, figs. 1 and 2). This seems to be an old type among the Senecas because it is present among collections made at the old Buffalo Creek reserve, Onondaga Valley, and Tonawanda; and one specimen is supposed to have been taken beyond the Niagara frontier into Canada before the Revolution (pl. 4, fig. 1). One such specimen was collected in Oklahoma, but it was probably taken there from Grand River, Ontario. These masks sometimes have a crest of spines on the forehead, but it is not a constant feature.

5. Masks with tongue protruding (dodänǫhgä'wɛh) as in pain were collected by DeCost Smith at Onondaga and by Lewis Morgan and David Boyle among the Onondaga of Grand River. It is relatively uncommon among the Senecas and may be considered an Onondaga type (pls. 5 and 6).

6. Not all the masks are wry-faced. Some of them are smiling (hoyóndiha'—he is smiling). As one informant remarked, "Maybe he saw a pretty girl and he is smiling." Smiling masks are frequently beggar masks, representations of the Common Faces of the forests. They are not confined to the Senecas of Coldspring, but the smiling masks from the Onondaga of Grand River are apt to be extremely heavy with thick, leering lips (pl. 7, fig. 2), a heavy chin,

and puffy cheeks; and some of these were unquestionably used in curing.

7. The whistler (hanǫ́·gaha‘) as his name implies has a puckered mouth, frequently enhanced by supplementary wrinkles. He is also called thebl owing spirit mask, or the Whistling God, Djinnaga'hihä‘. His likenesses occur among the Seneca and the Onondagas of Canada (pl. 8). They generally belong to the class of beggar or dancing masks and are not considered representations of the great world rim gods.

8. The divided mask represents a god whose body is riven in twain (dɛhodya'tgai·'ɛwɛ‘). According to Hewitt, who learned of him through Joshua Buck, his body is half human and half supernatural; hence his face is divided between deep red and pure black, symbolizing the east and the west, and he is free to wander at large even among the people. The Senecas, except a few at Tonawanda, are unfamiliar with him, and he seems to be a Cayuga-Onondaga spirit localized on Grand River where there are a few masks of him, which are not well known even there (pl. 9, fig. 1). It seems possible that the divided face concept was taken over from the Delaware who settled among the Cayuga.

9. *Other types of wooden masking.*—Longnose (hagǫ́nde's) masks are always taken as a joke by the Iroquois because they remind them of Longnose, the trickster, with whom they were threatened as naughty children (pl. 9, fig. 2). Probably very few of them were intended to represent the trickster, although such masks were anciently made of buckskin and later cloth to frighten children at Coldspring (pl. 10, fig. 2). A certain puckish wooden figure that stood before a Syracuse tobacconists, DeCost Smith was told, had inspired a few similar masks at Onondaga (pl. 10, fig. 1).

10. Horned masks (donǫ'gao·t—horns on it) are a relatively recent development at Newtown. According to Jesse Cornplanter, this so-called buffalo type of mask was first devised by Austin Jacobs about 1900, and since that time masks of this character have usurped roles that were formerly reserved for the "doctor" masks (pl. 11, fig. 1). Some of the horned masks have a decided diabolical or negroid appearance and were possibly intended as caricatures of white gods, or the other new race that came to live near the Senecas at Buffalo.

11. Animal masks are not as common among the Iroquois as among some primitives, and certainly they are few as compared with anthropomorphic likenesses. However, while I know of only one mask representing the Dew Eagle (S‘ada'ge'a·') or the Giant Raven (gáhgago·wa·), who is depicted as fetching in his bill the bloody scalp of the Good Hunter in the origin legend for the Little Water Society, masks representing the pig (gis'gwis) are fairly common

at Newtown (Seneca) and among the Cayuga of Grand River. At Newtown, James Crow formerly had a pig mask which was used as doorkeeper in a dream ceremonial constructed around the Delaware Skin-beating Dance. It is possible that pig masks are derived from masks representing the bear, but there is no evidence that such masks were used in the Bear Dance Society ritual. However, with the disappearance of the bear the pig has become the principal feast animal among the remnant Iroquois, and the pighead has acquired a reflected holiness by association with the rituals of the medicine societies (pl. 11, fig. 2). At Coldspring the pig is only a beggar mask who appears at the Midwinter Festival.

12. The blind mask (dágǫgwegǫ gagǫhsa') presents something of an enigma because it is either little known or informants are unwilling to discuss it. The former is apparently the reason because blind masks have been obsolete ceremonially for over a generation, according to J. Cornplanter, whose father remembered them from his youth. In the ritual of the I'do·s Medicine Society, the shaman demonstrated his power to see through the mask by juggling hot stones, and he knocked a standing doll from an inverted corn mortar. Furthermore, the masks of this ritual in the New York State Museum, which Parker published in 1909, do not appear to have had much use in ceremonies. Although a blind mask has been collected from the Seneca of Grand River (pl. 12), its use is unknown to my informants, the Gibsons. In this connection it is interesting that some Senecas think the black faces have more power because they usually have smaller eye holes than the red ones, but other informants say red masks are equally powerful, and James Crow said that to meet a red one might cause nosebleed. At any rate the red and black masks are about equally represented in our collections.

The husk faces or "bushy-heads."—Besides the wooden False-faces, corn husk masks represent another class of earth-bound supernatural beings who formed a pact with mankind and taught them the arts of hunting and agriculture. The techniques of twining and braiding corn husks in the manufacture of shoes, mats, and dishes is ancient among the Iroquois peoples, and it is one of the traits that point to a southern origin for those elements of their culture that are associated with the cultivation of maize. Nevertheless, the use of husk masks is probably no older than sewing braided corn husks for seats and foot mats, since the Husk Faces and the beings which they represent are named like the mats "bushy, fuzzy, or awry" (gadji·'sa'). The husk faces look like door mats, the only difference being that the masks have holes for the eyes and mouth and the pile is cut off on the inside, but they too have a ragged fringe of hair. Thus a person awaking with his hair standing awry, like the pile of a foot mat, in said to look like gadji·'sa'—a bushy-head.

Three techniques of manufacture produce as many types of husk masks. Most commonly long strips of corn husk braid are sewn in three coils which form the eyes and mouth, and the nose and fringe are added. The females of the species are designated by appending little knobs of covered husk to the fringe, eyes, and nose. The rougher looking ones are considered old men and the smoother ones are youths (pl. 13). Usually the mouths are small and round, but again they take on the mouth shapes of the Wooden Faces. At Grand River, husk faces are more coarsely braided and more completely cover the wearer (pl. 14, fig. 2).

Twined husk faces were until recently made by old Seneca women at Allegany, and at Cattaraugus only one old woman still makes them. The technique of twining involves twisting a pair of wefts around each radiating warp as it is passed until one reaches the rim of the mask. Twined masks are commenced at the nose (pl. 14, fig. 1). The poorly made ones with stubble on the cheeks are grandfathers, and the smooth-faced "bushy-heads" with a round red spot painted on each cheek are young people bound for religious festivals at the longhouse.

Among the Onondaga of Grand River, Canada, besides the masks made entirely of corn husks or wood, there is a third variety known as wooden bushy-head (owɛ''ga gadji·'sa'). This is a natural wood mask with undistorted human features having only ceremonial face painting confined to a round red spot on each cheek or a series of vertical lines beneath the lower lip. It has corn husk fringe as hair, and is credited with more power than the other husk faces (pl. 15, fig. 1).

Miniature masks.—For all the larger varieties of masks there seem to be miniature masks which take the characteristic types and art styles of the localities where they are made. These are either kept as personal charms or they are hung on the larger masks and "ride along" in the ceremonies (pl. 15, fig. 2).

HISTORICAL PERSPECTIVE

Archeology.—Stone faces and faces on pots and pipes occur in sufficient abundance throughout the historic area of the Iroquois to lead one to suspect that the prehistoric Iroquois entertained conceptions of supernatural beings like those which their historic descendants associate with the False-faces. The appearance of some of the human and animal faces modeled on the bowls of earthenware pipes, usually to face the smoker, suggests that they were intended to represent wooden masks. However, the archeological evidence further confirms an inference that we can make from the accounts of early travelers below, namely, that the False-face rituals made their appearance among the Seneca of western New York relatively late in the seventeenth century considerably after they were first observed by the French at Huronia, because Wintemberg and Parker find that a type of pipe known as the "blowing face" was first evolved during the post-European period of Neutral, Huron, Tionontati, and Seneca culture.[21] Furthermore, during the colonial period the clay pipes were imitated in stone, and such a pipe with a blowing spirit mask facing the smoker has turned up recently near a late historic sugaring campsite of the Cornplanter band of Senecas (pl. 16).

Narratives of early travelers.—From the earliest European contacts with the Huron and Iroquois over 3 centuries ago, the explorers and missionaries, while they do not always specifically mention masks, at least describe ceremonies that are now connected with masks in the modern rituals. The behavior of the actors is older than the form of the masks, and it would seem that the ritualized Iroquois masked shamanism that we observe in practice today has kept alive old tricks of the Huron Oki or medicine man, who was not always masked. The Oki handled hot coals and blew ashes on his patient, and Champlain (1616) witnessed the hysterical frenzy of medicine men and neurotic women who walked "on all fours like beasts" until the masked company were summoned to displace their possession by blowing upon them to the din of their turtle rattles; and they "parade the length of the village while the feast is being prepared for the masquers, who return very tired, having taken enough exercise to empty the kettle of its Migan."[22] In another place he describes the beggar maskers, men and women, visiting each other's villages much as they now go from house to house at Midwinter. In 1623 Gabriel Sagard, whom Champlain invited to spend an exciting winter in Huronia, found the Okis still in business, and he witnessed an unmistakable example of the doorkeeper's role in the modern ritual. The actor wore a bearskin garb reminiscent of those in use among Delaware and Onondaga maskers of recent times, although a wooden mask is not mentioned.

I have seen . . . a bear skin covering the whole body, the ears erect on top of their head, their face covered up except for the eyes; and these persons were only acting as doorkeepers or jesters and took no part in the dance except at intervals, because they were for a different purpose.[23]

---

[21] Wintemberg, W. J., Distinguishing characteristics of Algonkian and Iroquoian cultures. Nat. Mus. Canada, Ann. Rep. 1929, p. 78, Ottawa, 1931; Roebuck prehistoric village site . . . Nat. Mus. Canada, Bull. 83, p. 75, 1936; Parker, A. C., The archeological history of New York. New York State Mus. Bull. 235, p. 146, 1922.

[22] Champlain, Samuel de, Voyages . . ., vol. 3, pp. 153–155. The Champlain Society, Toronto, 1929.

[23] Sagard, Father Gabriel, The long journey to the country of the Hurons, p. 117. The Champlain Society, Toronto, 1939.

Furthermore, as now at Grand River, the patient was also led around in the medicine dance and encouraged to recover, and there was a terminal feast for invited guests.

While these descriptions do not fit the modern ceremonies precisely, they at least contain the kernels out of which the modern rituals have grown.

For the Iroquois of New York at this period we do not find accounts of face painting and masking, comparing the Indians with the masqueraders in the French Mardi Gras. However, the author of Van Curler's journal, whose party visited the Mohawk villages and the Oneida town at Christmas of 1634, tells us how on two occasions the Chief of the first Mohawk Castle ". . . showed me his idol; it was a head with the teeth sticking out; it was dressed in a red cloth." [24] This is reminiscent of the modern custom of covering masks when putting them away. A fortnight later at Oneida, he saw a dozen red-faced Oneida shamans handle and eat fire while attempting to drive away evil spirits to the accompaniment of a turtle rattle.

The "Relations" for 1636 and 1637 mention the antics of the False-faces and their husk-face doorkeepers among the Huron. Brebeuf [25] writes, that in the Midwinter Festival of 1636:

> You would have seen some with a sack on the head, pierced only for the eyes; others were stuffed with straw around the middle, to imitate a pregnant woman. Several were naked as the hand . . .

And so do the modern maskers go naked to the waist. The following December at the great Huron village of Ossosané ". . . they donned their masks and danced, to drive away the disease." [26] During this winter a clairvoyant came into prominence among the Hurons, and his name Tsondacoüanné is not only preserved to us in the "Relations," but my informants identify it with their term for the individual who sponsors a medicine feast (godęsoni—she sponsored the ritual; sadęsoni—you . . . sponsor). In a dance which he ordered [to drive away pestilence—

> All the dancers were disguised as hunchbacks, with wooden masks which were altogether ridiculous, and each had a stick in his hand. An excellent medicine, forsooth! At the end of the dance, at the command of the sorcerer Tsondacoüane all these masks were hung at the end of poles, and placed over every cabin, with the straw men at the doors, to frighten the malady . . . [p. 263].

And a day or so later they beat upon pieces of bark, making a great din, and a householder burned tobacco and urged the masks to keep

---

[24] Wilson, James Grant, Arent Van Curler and his journal. Ann. Rep. Amer. Hist. Assoc. for 1895, pp. 88, 95, 1896.
[25] Jesuit Relations (Thwaites edition), vol. 10, p. 203.
[26] Op cit., vol. 13, p. 175.

a good watch over his door (p. 267). Another time all the houses in the environs of a neighboring town were decked out with wooden masks and straw figures within 48 hours of the sorcerer's edict (p. 231).

Surely, if these practices had been current among the Five Nations of New York at this time, the Jesuits who visited them during the next few decades would have mentioned the masked ceremonies which they knew from Huronia. Instead, Dablon and Chaumonot, who witnessed the Midwinter Festival at Onondaga during 1656, are silent about masks but describe their host, covering himself with corn husks from head to foot, who went accompanied by two women with blackened faces and bodies covered with wolf skins. Each woman carried a club or a great stake.[27] Beschefer, who accompanied De Nonville's expedition against the Seneca, wrote in the "Relations" of 1687 to Villermont:

> I was mistaken when I told you that the Iroquois wore no masks. They make some very hideous ones with pieces of wood, which they carve according to their fancy. When our people burned the villages of the Tsonnontouans (Seneca), a young man made every effort in his power to get one that an outaouae (Ottawa) had found in a cabin, but the latter would not part with it. It was a foot and a half long, and wide in proportion; 2 pieces of a kettle, very neatly fitted to it, and pierced with a small hole in the center, represented the eyes.[28]

Beauchamp holds that since the Seneca had one Huron town after 1648, the Huron may have introduced the False-face Society to the Seneca, from whence it spread through the other nations of the Confederacy. Lafitau, who bolstered his Mohawk observation with the earlier "Jesuit Relations," says masks were made from the bark of trees.[29] John Bartram, the Philadelphia naturalist, recorded an unmistakable description of a False-face beggar who kept him awake at Onondaga in 1743.

> ... we were entertained by a comical fellow, disguised in as odd a dress as Indian folly could invent; he had on a clumsy vizard of wood colour'd black, with a nose 4 or 5 inches long, a grinning mouth set awry, furnish'd with long teeth, round the eyes circles of bright brass, surrounded by a larger circle of white paint, from his forehead hung long tresses of buffaloes hair, and from the catch part of his head ropes made of the plaited husks of Indian corn; I can not recollect the whole of his dress, but that it was equally uncouth: he carried in one hand a long staff, in the other a calabash with small stones in it, for a rattle, and this he rubbed up and down his staff; he would sometimes hold up his head and make a hideous noise like the braying of an ass; ... In my whim I saw a vizard of this kind hang by the side of one of their cabins to another town.[30]

---

[27] Op. cit., vol. 42, p. 154.
[28] Op. cit., vol. 63, p. 289.
[29] Lafitau, P. F., Moeurs des sauvages Amériquains, vol. 1, p. 368. Paris, 1724.
[30] Bartram, John, Observations on the inhabitants, climate, soil, rivers, productions, animals ... in Travels from Pennsylvania (sic) to Onondaga, Oswego and Lake Ontario, p. 43. London, 1751 (reprinted at Geneva, N. Y., 1895).

Probably a custom as widespread over the world as dressing in masks to impersonate other beings permits us to assume that the Iroquoian custom of wearing false faces sprang from their own or Huron culture whence it spread to the Iroquois after 1648, where it became so firmly imbedded that, despite 300 years of buffeting by white contact, the masks have maintained standards prescribed in the origin legends. The masks show little fundamental change from generation to generation, except that they become increasingly ornate and grotesque when influenced by the adoption of better tools or the degeneration of the wood-carver's art; and masks portraying a pig, the devil, and such amusing figures as Mickey Mouse, Felix Cat, and Charlie Chaplin have encroached only on the group of faces designed to elicit laughter—the class of beggar masks—which is the most plastic.

THE SOCIETY OF HUSK FACES OR BUSHY-HEADS

The Husk Faces are a race of agriculturists. They dwell on the other side of the earth in a ravine where they till their fields amid high stumps. Coming from the east every new year, they visit the Seneca longhouses during 2 nights of the Midwinter Festival. Preceded by runners, they finally arrive amid a great din of beating the building with staves, stop the dances, and kidnap a chief for interpreter. As messengers of the three sisters—corn, beans, and squash—our life supporters, they have great powers of prophecy. The interpreter relates the message of the old woman, their leader, that they are hurrying westward to hoe their crops. In fields about their houses they grow huge squashes; the corn has giant ears, and string beans climb up poles to heaven. Some of their women have remained home to tend to crying babies. Recently in their country there is employment on public works projects. These statements are accepted as an augury of fertility. They request the privilege of dancing with the people. All their company may be men, but some dress as women and participate in the dances as if they were women.

The Husk Face Society is by no means as well integrated or prominent as the False-face Society, although they share certain functions. Unlike the False-faces, they are mutes and only puff as they run with great leaps. They have their own tobacco invocation, a medicine song, and they dance about the staves which they carry. They also have the power to cure by blowing hot ashes; but in Canada they sprinkle water on their patients. They like tobacco, but they prefer popcorn at Allegany and dumplings at Newtown and Tonawanda, instead of mush. When four suddenly appear racing between the houses, they may be signaling the approach of the False-face Company. They will loiter, policing the premises until the Common Faces depart. Relatively few Indians belong to their society, and set a kettle down for them to renew an old dream, but many put on their masks for the public longhouse rituals, and others join them in social dances at the end of the line.

Origin of the Onondaga Husk Faces.—Hadji‸'să (for Gaji‸'să'), the Man-being of the Corn Husk Likeness [Mask]—a Tradition of the Olden Time.[31]

(It is said) that in ancient times it thus happened that a man who was hunting in the forest saw there while on the hunt something. He was surprised to see there a deer standing at the bottom of a valley. He killed it. When he had completed dressing the carcass he looked as he turned around and saw standing there nearby a male Husk Face and he asked him, saying, "Where do you come from?" He replied, "From the place where the uprooted tree trunk is."

Again the hunter asked, "Where then are you going?" He answered, "Only thy person too do I come seeking. I am bearing corn. Expressly for thee[you] am I bringing it." He had brought two ears of corn. The hunter then asked, "From what place do you bring it?" He replied, "On the farther side of the bushes one has planted it. Odendonni″a‛ (The Sapling or Sprout: a name for the Life God or the Master of Life) has planted that.

"He planted it for you (human beings). It belongs to you (people). I have come bringing it for thee. You must mix it with what you are hunting, when you do eat.

"He himself, gaende″sǫ'k (Moving Winds) sent me from there, and also Otcgǫwendet″ha' (The Tempest)." He said, "You go deliver the corn. The hunter will carry it back to the people when he returns home! That is the reason I deliver it to you. You must take it home.

"Whole Face Man-being (gaende″sǫ'k), accompanied me. Customarily, I go there [about the houses] when again as usual [whenever] the humpbacked man beings (hoñdu″i') again go about from place to place.

"I have my dwelling place where berries are wont to grow. There in that place usually I pick up corn bread, when [once more] you human beings are gathering berries again. Ordinarily, I take the corn bread which is brought there as provisions. But you [people] never see me.

"Understand that I have dwelt on the earth from the beginning with the Master of Life. I am independent (wild). You must tell your people that you and they must prepare something with corn husks which shall be a likeness of the form of my body. And it shall be that when they wear this husk mask that wearing the mask will enable me to aid them. Understand that it is I who will bring to you [people] all the seeds which you will plant—seed corn, seed beans, and squash seed. All the various kinds of seeds will I deliver in full. I will bring them from the many planted fields of the Sapling (or Sprout—Odeñdoñni'a‛— a name for the Master of Life). So then don't let anyone complain of the amount of the seeds which I shall bring (to maturity). Understand also that it is Diyos'a″di‛ (i. e., Producer of all Things), the Mother of the Sprout, who brought them here for us to gather.

"Therefore, appropriately (customarily) when one will have thoughts concerning me than one shall usually say 'Djohgwe″yani' Hadji'śa' (Mr. Partridge Bushy-head).'

"So now you alone must carry home with you all the things which I have given you."

---

[31] The native Onondaga-Iroquoian text was dictated June 1916 by Joshua Buck, a Tutelo-Onondaga, of the Six Nations Grant on the Grand River, Ontario, and later revised and translated with notes by J. N. B. Hewitt.

Longnose, who kidnaps naughty children.—The Iroquois and their Algonquin neighbors use buckskin masks to impersonate cannibal clowns who sometimes kidnap naughty children. The Seneca call this clown "Longnose" (hagónde·s) because of his elongated proboscis. He is the Indian bogeyman. He chases bad children when the old people are sleeping. He mimics them, crying out as he runs after them. But the old folks do not wake up, since he has bewitched them in order that they will remain sleeping. This goes on all night until the child gives up and agrees to behave, or else Longnose makes away with the child, carrying him off in a huge pack basket. It is not right to whip little children. Stubborn children who will not go to bed are sometimes sent out at dusk to meet Longnose, impersonated by a relative wearing a cloth mask. The child immediately runs into the house. Neither is it right to use the great wooden masks belonging to the medicine society for scaring little children. The great Faces are sacred and should not be ridiculed; and the being they represent might, through the mask, "poison" the child, or "spoil his face" and bring bad luck to the wearer.

The Bigheads.—At the Seneca Midwinter Festival, two women dress two men in buffalo robes, which they bind with ropes of braided corn husks, from which the ears have been successively pulled for consumption; they hand the men wooden corn pounders and dispatch them about the village. These heralds impersonate the "Uncles" or "Bigheads" who run through the fires heralding the Feast of Dreams which marks the new year. Their costume symbolizes the union of trophies of the hunt and fruit of the harvest. The Bigheads should not be confused with the wooden False-faces or the Husk Faces, who form two distinct but somewhat linked medicine companies.

THE SOCIETY OF FACES, OR THE FALSE-FACE COMPANY

The origin of the False-faces.—Among the Iroquois there are two prevailing types of origin legends for the wooden False-faces. One is a mythical epic belonging to the creation; the other is a human adventure. Both are associated with different classes of beings. In abridged form, here is what Chauncey Johnny John and Henry Redeye heard from their "old folks."

THE STRUGGLE FOR CONTROL OF THE EARTH

Now when our maker was finishing this earth, he went walking around inspecting it and banishing all evil spirits from his premises. He divested the Stonecoats and banished them as harmful to men. He removed the Little Folk's stone shirts and permitted them to remain to help hunters and cure illness. As the creator went on his way westward, on the rim of the world, he met a huge fellow—the head man of all the Faces. The creator asked the stranger, as he had asked the others, whence he came. The stranger replied that he came from the Rocky Mountains to the west and that he had been living on this earth since he made it. They argued as to whose earth they traversed and agreed to settle the title by contest. The creator agreed to call the stranger "headman," should he demonstrate sufficient magic strength to summon a distant mountain toward them. They sat down facing the east with their backs to the west and held their breath. Now the great False-face shook his giant turtle rattle and the uproar freightened the game animals. He summoned the mountain toward them, but it moved only part way. Now it was the creator's turn, and he summoned the mountain, which came directly up to them. However, his rival, becoming impatient, suddenly looked around, and the mountain struck his face. The impact broke his nose bridge, and pain distorted his mouth. Now the creator realized that this fellow had great power. He assigned him the task of driving disease from the earth and assisting the people who were about to travel to and fro hunting. The loser agreed that if humans make portrait masks of him, call him grandfather, make tobacco offerings, and set down a kettle of mush, that they too shall have the power to cure disease by blowing hot ashes. The creator gave him a place to dwell in the rocky hills to the west near the rim of the earth, and he agreed to come in whichever direction the people summon him.

The Good Hunter's Adventure

Later, as humans went about the earth, in the fall men went into the woods hunting. They carried native tobacco and parched corn meal for mush. They were tormented by shy, querulous beings who flitted timidly behind trees with their long hair snapping in the wind. Sometimes a hunter returned to his camp to find the ashes of his fire strewn about the hearth and the marks of some great, dirty hand where someone had grasped a house post for support as he leaned over and pawed in the fire. The hunter agreed to stay home while his partner went afield. During the morning, a False-face approached cautiously, sledging on one hip, now and then standing erect to gaze about before proceeding. Going to the hearth, he reached into the ashes and scattered the coals as if seeking something. That night the hunter had a dream in which the False-face requested tobacco and mush. The next day, the hunter set a kettle down for them. The Faces came and taught him their songs and their method of treating patients with hot ashes. In a subsequent dream, they requested him to remember them every year with a feast, saying they are everywhere in the forests, bringing luck to those who remember them.

Another legend from Chauncey Johnny John tells of a hunter who inadvisedly shot but failed to kill an old man whom he discovered sitting on a log in the forest. The man returned the arrow, instructed the hunter to make 100 bark bowls, to cook a great kettle of mush, and provide tobacco for a company of 100 who would appear next day. The amazed hunter fulfilled everything, and when he was ready, Faces of all ages gathered around his fire. The old man, who was their leader, taught him a tobacco invocation and three songs. They showed him how to cure by blowing hot ashes, and presented him with a miniature mask to serve as a model for making larger ones.

Hunters returned home to their villages. They related their strange adventures and revealed their dreams. Sometimes after returning home, they had new dreams and received further instructions. They showed their people how to make masks and they organized a medicine company.

THE CLASSES OF MEDICINE MASKS

Rationalizing from the two types of origin legends, the modern Iroquois conceive two main classes of False-faces: First, their leader, the great fellow who lived on the rim of the earth, and secondly, his underlings, the common forest people whose faces are against the trees. The great one, called shagodyowêhgo·wa· [hadjá'dot'a', "Our defender the doctor," in Seneca, and "The great humpbacked one (hadu"i'go·na')" by the Onondaga, is the greatest 'doctor. He is earth-bound and traverses the earth from east to west following the path of the sun. He is tall and carries a great staff, made from a giant pine or shagbark hickory tree with its branches lopped off to the top. He walks with great strides, bumping his cane and shaking the earth. He carries a huge mud-turtle rattle, and he stops at noon to rest and rub his rattle on the giant elm or pine which stand in the center of the earth and from which he derives great strength (pl. 17, fig. 1). His face is red in the morning as he comes from the east, but black in the afternoon as he looks back from the direction of the setting sun. He controls high winds and has a wary eye for pestilences which might destroy the people. He has a song which refers to his power over winds and pestilence. Few have ever seen him. He dances, kicking out his feet and sparring, his thumbs pointed in the air as if he were about to fall over backward. He makes the people imitate him, organizes them in a round dance, and watches the door to see that no one leaves or enters. Masks representing him have long hair. They are painted red or black and portray the broken nose and pain he suffered when the mountain struck his face. A few masks have high-bridged noses, and all have protruding lips, which are twisted with the nose, straight, hanging, or flaring like two funnels or flattened like spoons, for blowing ashes.

The second class are the Common Faces, who live everywhere in the forests (pl. 17, fig. 2). They are deformed, either hunchbacked or crippled below the waist. Some carry rattles, made by folding a rind of hickory bark; a few possess turtle rattles, but others have only a stick. They crave mush and beg for tobacco. They have a dance and a song, and they will cure by blowing hot ashes. Masks of this category are ill-defined and include a great variety. Frequently new masks make their debut with the Common Faces; but after they have been worn in many rituals, borrowed and passed through the hands of several owners, they will have accumulated several bags of tobacco offerings, attained an antique color, and achieved sufficient prestige to graduate into the class of great doctor masks where their sanctity is preserved by reputation.

THREE SOCIETIES EMPLOY MASKS

Among the Iroquois, three distinct medicine societies employ masks. They perform their rituals in public or privately. The False-face Company, who wear the wooden masks, include both orders of medicine masks who have three distinct rituals. Their public rituals are the spring and autumn exorcism of disease from the settlements and cures which are sometimes sponsored in the longhouse during the Midwinter Festival. However, the public appearance of the Beggars and Thieves, during several nights of the midwinter ceremonies, are merely a motely group of boys who sometimes "take sick" afterward and thereby gain admittance to the society (pl. 18, fig. 1). The second ritual belongs to the Common Faces, who enter a house and dance (pls. 19, 20). The Common Faces may be followed by the great, world-rim Faces, whose ritual is the Doorkeeper's Dance. The Society of Faces is the body of people who have been cured by the masked company. The separate society of Husk Faces appears publicly two nights at the Midwinter Festival. They have their own invocation, songs, and a curing dance. Membership is gained by a dream or cure, but nonmembers join in their public dances, dancing at the end of the line. Frequently at Allegany two special Husk Faces appear as doorkeepers for the Common Faces at private curing rites and as heralds and longhouse police during public rituals. Among the Canadian Iroquois, masked societies seem more highly specialized, but at Allegany and Tonawanda their functions are less clearly defined. At Newtown, on Cattaraugus reserve, the Society of Mystic Animals (hadi″do·s) possess certain "secret masks" of which one has no eye holes, but at Coldspring on Allegany Reservation certain black or white Faces, which are also used as medicine masks by the Society of Faces, appear in one ritual of the Society of Mystic Animals and juggle hot stones or hot ashes while curing the patient (pl. 18, fig. 2).

Membership.—An Iroquois Indian joins a particular medicine society after a dream or because a clairvoyant has prescribed the ritual of that society to cure a sickness. He automatically joins all the societies, and is afterward duty bound to sponsor any combination of rituals that have assisted his recovery. Thus the Society of Faces includes persons who have been cured by the False-face Company. Membership in the several orders of the society, or participation in the rituals of the masked company depend on an individual's personal history. The masked company are men wearing masks of the orders which cured them, but both men and women sponsor the rituals and belong to the orders that have accepted them for membership in the society by making them sick. Among the Seneca, two head women, one from each moiety of four clans, are responsible for certain equipment and manage the rituals. Members of both sexes attend. A member should put up a feast every year for the orders which have helped him. He calls in the head woman of the opposite moiety to conduct the ritual. His membership ceases rarely, when he dreams he has been released. Then he knows he is no longer a member.

THE FALSE-FACE SICKNESS

Symptoms of the False-face sickness are ailments of the head, shoulders, and joints. Masks cause and cure swelling of the face, toothache, inflammation of the eyes, nose bleeding, sore chin, and earache. At Tonawanda, red spots on the patient's face are False-face symptoms. This calls for the red Faces, who should dance in the morning before sunrise. Black spots require the use of black masks at night. Imaginary hair lying on the patient's face, indicated by her attempts to brush it aside, is a False-face symptom. The patient complains to her old people. They consult a clairvoyant, who prescribes a False-face ceremony. To ridicule the masks or any of their ceremonies is inviting sickness or misfortune.

Cases of hysterical possession formerly occurred among Iroquois women. A Tonawanda informant states that it was confined to certain nervous women who became possessed of the False-face spirits whenever the masked men appeared (Peter W. Doctor). On hearing the rumpus of whining and rattles, which marks their approach, one woman would fall into spasms, imitate their cry and crawl toward the fire, and, unless she was restrained, plunge her hands into the glowing embers and scatter the fire as if she were a False-face hunting tobacco. Some one always grabbed her, while another burned tobacco, imploring the masked men to cure her. The ritual usually restored her normal composure. Other women became possessed of the tutelaries of the Bear or Buffalo societies. My informant used to think women became possessed to show off. Some of these women were clairvoyants. Another informant remembers a man who became possessed 30 years ago at Newtown, for resisting a doorkeeper (Jesse J. Cornplanter). When the masked ritual conductor nudged him with his rattle, he obstinately refused to join the round dance. They struggled and the man, overcome with fear, fell into a spasm and cried like a False-face. They had to blow ashes on him. Afterward, the man did not remember his behavior. In all cases, the form of the hysteria was prescribed by the culture. These cases resemble those which Champlain and the missionaries witnessed at Huronia. The Feast of Fools of the early Hurons has evolved from a random series of hysterical dream fulfillments to an organized Midwinter Festival by a gradual standardization of forms differing according to locality.

THE MASK AND RATTLE

Men belonging to the Society of Faces usually own a bundle containing a turtle rattle and one or more masks decorated with bags of sacred tobacco. When not being used, the mask is laid away, face down with its hair wreathed around the face and the turtle shell placed in the hollow at the back of the mask; and the whole is wrapped in the cloth head cover. Sometimes unwrapped masks are hung upstairs, but facing the wall. A mask hung facing out should be covered, lest some frightened persons become possessed and join the society. One must be careful of them. If a mask falls, the owner burns a tobacco offering and ties a little bundle of sacred tobacco at the ear or forehead. Whenever he dreams about the Face, he will rise and repeat the ritual. Every man has a package of tobacco on his mask which he removes when he sells it to white people. He burns tobacco, telling the mask that it is going away. He asks it not to return and harm him or the new owner (pl. 21, fig. 2). Everyone belonging to the society may use anyone else's face. A new owner will add a package of tobacco to a mask, and if he purchases one already having several attached medicine bundles, he adds his own; but a maker does not tie tobacco on a mask unless he intends to keep and use it. Sometimes the masks become hungry and the owners rub their lips with mush and anoint their faces with sunflower oil, which after many years imparts a rich luster. A man, having no children, may request that a mask be buried with him.

Unless the new member inherits an old mask, he must carve one or enlist the services of a carver. They say at Tonawanda that softer woods are best for carving masks. Basswood has the prestige of tradition, but other soft woods like willow and cucumber are also used. Anciently, a man went into the forest to carve his masks. He carried native tobacco and sought a living basswood tree. Now he committed the tobacco to the burning embers, a pinch at a time, addressing his prayer to the tree and the beings whom the False-faces represent. Then he carved the face on the living tree (pl. 21, fig. 1), and having roughed it out, he notched the tree with an ax above the forehead and below the chin and cleaved away his sculpture in a solid block. It is said that the carving never broke because one had put tobacco and asked the tree for its life. Nor did the tree die. Within 4 years, the scar healed over. He took home his block, covered it and worked on it at his leisure. When the features were finished, he hollowed out the inside (with a bent farrier's knife), and perforated the eyes, nose, and mouth (pl. 22). He encircled the eyes with metal, for the Great False-face's eyes are bright. Then he painted it. If he had sought his tree in the morning, he painted the mask red; but if he found the tree and commenced carving after noon, the mask would be black. This color symbolism originates with the theory of morning and afternoon appearance of the giant, world-rim resident. During his daily westward journey following the path of the sun, his face would appear red in the morning and dark in the afternoon when the sun is behind him. For the long hair which falls on either side to his knees, the mask maker attaches to the forehead horsetails, tanned with deer brains.

RITUAL EQUIPMENT

The False-face Company carry wooden staves and employ three instruments: The typical mud-turtle rattle, a folded bark rattle, or a billet of wood. On late spring evenings, before summer heat peels the turtle's shell, Indians watch for turtles about the ponds and creeks. In the evening one may meet an Indian bearing a burlap sack containing a turtle, or he carries it by the tail; he is bound to the house of a friend who "can fix it" for a rattle. The rattle maker cuts off the turtle's tail or severs the jugular vein and hangs it to drain. Later, he eviscerates and cures it. He sews up the apertures left by removing the rear limbs and inserts a handful of cherry pits. He stretches the neck over a pine stick which extends from inside the shell to the base of the skull where it is notched. He sews the front rents. Cutting three hickory splints, he inserts one in the sternum, cutting it off under the jaw, and he inserts two lateral splints in the back of the shell, terminating them on top of the head. He binds the splints to the neck with basswood fiber, a withe of inner elm bark, or rawhide, commencing at the shell and whipping toward the head. A ten-inch rattle is best for singing, but the mammoth turtle rattles lend awe to the doorkeepers at curing rites and small turtle rattles furnish comedy for little boys playing beggars (pl. 23, fig. 1).

For the bark rattles, a cylinder of green hickory bark is slit longitudinally and peeled around the tree. The maker spreads it at the middle by inserting his thumbs and folds it end to end, placing one curled end inside the other (pl. 23, fig. 2). A few cherry pits, pebbles, or kernels of corn provide the necessary percussion. He plugs the open end with a corncob and lashes it with a bark withe. A man will make a dozen on a summer afternoon and toss them overhead in the loft to dry.

At next Midwinter Festival, a band of outlandishly dressed little boys wearing beggar masks may visit him soliciting or pilfering food and tobacco for a feast. He will reward them, and then, reaching overhead, distribute his rattles to those poor youngsters who were unable to locate turtle rattles and carry sticks of kindling. Perhaps he has no children of his own. He will sing for them and they will dance and depart.

A rattle borrowed from a dancer or a stick of wood is good enough to beat time for the dances. But despite the Indians' ingenuity to makeshift of anything at hand the False-face Company sometimes possess dance-tempo beaters. They range in design from wooden cudgels to elaborately carved wooden turtles that have been hollowed to house noisy pebbles. These wooden replicas of the genuine turtle rattles exemplify the transfer to an artistic medium of a design originating with a structural invention.

Miniature masks.—Boys sometimes learn by carving miniature masks. The mask may make the owner ill and then he joins the society. Masquettes are also charms to protect dwellings against witchcraft, or they hang on larger masks. A man may carve one in response to a dream and carry it for good luck. At Cattaraugus, the leader of the society carries a striped pole on which a tobacco basket, a small wooden face, a tiny husk face and a diminutive mud-turtle rattle hang near the top. This is her staff of office when she leads the masked company from house to house exorcising plagues.

Spring and autumn house cleaning.—In the spring and fall, when sickness lingers in the settlements, a great company, wearing both classes of medicine masks, go through the houses frightening disease spirits. At Coldspring, two groups start at opposite sides of the settlement. They are preceded by Husk Face runners. Members take down their masks and rattles and join the procession as it passes. The masked exterminators frequently strip to the waist and go armed with rattles to scare the spirit of sickness and carry pine boughs to brush away malefic influences. A believer is said to suffer no injury from plunging his bare hands into the fire nor become sick from exposure while traveling in cold weather. One winter at Allegany the company afforded a wild spectacle as they sped up the valley road in open Fords with their hair whipping in the chill winds; they grated their rattles on the car body and uttered their terrifying cries whenever they swerved to pass a stranger. Approaching houses occupied by members of the society, an unmasked leader sings:

> A long voice, A long voice
> yowige yowige wige

and on again entering the longhouse:

> It might happen, It might happen
> ha i ge ha i
> From the mighty Shagodyoweh
> ha i ge he i
> I shall derive good luck
> ha i ge he i

He hopes that the great one dwelling on the rim of the earth will confer his power on the masked company and prevent high winds from leveling the settlement. They scour the exterior of the house and, crawling through the door, visit every room. They sweep beneath the beds and peer into every nook and corner for disease spirits. They haul the sick out of bed and sometimes commit indignities on lazy people. If someone has set a kettle down for them, their leader will burn tobacco, and ask the masked company to blow ashes on the patient. Their only fee is native tobacco, which their guide collects in a twined husk basket. Once at Newtown, a leader was about to gather his company of exterminators and depart for another house when one turned up missing. They heard a most terrifying racket in the loft. They ascended to discover him violently shaking an old straw bedticking, from which bedbugs were fleeing by the score. This fellow, now an old man, possessed of an extraordinary sense of the ridiculous, was shaking his rattle and crying in the most orthodox manner. It is a good example of the frivolity which may pervade an otherwise serious ritual.

Meanwhile, the two matrons brew a purgative at the village cook house. At Newtown and Tonawanda, the sole ingredient is parched white sunflower seeds, which are steeped for the medicine, but at Allegany they add "manroot" (*Ipomoea pandurata*), which must be found growing erect like a living person.

The community assembles at the longhouse. An appointed speaker returns thanks to all the spirit forces. At Coldspring, Husk Face runners and the marching song signify the approach of the combined company. Bursting into the room, the False-faces crawl toward the fire. Each matron entrusts a pail of medicine to one of them whom she designates "water waiter" for her moiety. Lest they scatter the fire about the room, an appointed priest makes an invocation, burning the tobacco that was levied at the houses. He implores them to protect the people against epidemics and tornadoes.

Tobacco Invocation

Partake of this sacred tobacco, O mighty shagodyoweh, you who live at the rim of the earth, who stand towering, you who travel everywhere on the earth caring for the people.

And you too, whose faces are against the trees in the forests, whom we call the company of faces; you also receive tobacco.

And you Husk Faces partake of the tobacco. For you have been continually associated with the False-faces. You too have done your duty.

Partake of this tobacco together. Everyone here believes that you have chosen him for your society.

So now your mud-turtle rattle receives tobacco. (Here they scrape their rattles on the floor.)

And now another thing receives tobacco, your staff, a tall pine with the branches lopped off to the top.

So presently you will stand up (they crawl in) and help your grandchildren, since they have fulfilled your desires. Fittingly, they have set down a full kettle of mush for you. It is greased with bear fat. Now another thing is fulfilled: on top there are strips of fried meat as large as your feet. (Here the False-faces roll in ecstacy on their backs, grasping their feet, peering at them, and attempting to put them in their mouths.) Besides, a brimming kettle of hulled-corn soup rests here.

Now it is up to you. Arise and help your grandchildren. They have fulfilled everything that you requested should be done here. In my opinion we have these ashes here for you to use. Arise and make medicine.

Here the priest summons those who wish to be cured to come forward and stand near the fire to receive the administrations of the False-faces.

The masked waiters pass the medicine water. Every one drinks all he can. Two Husk Faces watch the doors to insure that no one leaves or enters during the imbibing. However, they can sometimes be bribed with a pinch of tobacco.

There are dances for each class of Faces. An appointed singer straddles a bench, and borrowing a rattle, sings for the Common Faces alone. They stand up and dance and apply hot ashes to any patients whose dreams have required that they be cured on this occasion. Frequently, little boys who are wearing masks have to be held up by their elders in order to blow ashes on the patients' heads. Sometimes, a clever little fellow will puff the ashes at the patient from his upturned hand. At Tonawanda, the masked dancers cure each other. A matron distributes tobacco and they depart with their kettle of mush.

Next the Husk Faces perform, receive popcorn, and bound out of the room.

The second part of the ritual, named "They place one foot ahead of the other" for one of its component dances, includes the Dance of the Doorkeepers. The song commences. Two men, who are appointed from opposite moieties, appear wearing the medicine masks representing the great world-rim beings. They dance with the matrons, each facing the woman of the other moiety. A couple dances in unison, hopping on the left foot while bending the right knee and then kicking out the right foot. At the same time they spar at each other with the extended left hand, pointing the thumb upward. The turtle rattles dangle by the loop on the handle. Now the matrons pair the men and women in couples who dance imitating the False-faces. They spar at each other and a bold woman will sometimes back a bashful man from the floor. A doorkeeper looks inside once during each song (pl. 24).

Then they return and compel everyone inside to join a round dance, from which the ritual takes its name, since a dancer lifts his foot, bumps his heel and sets it down again ahead of the other.

One doorkeeper directs the dance, while his cousin watches the door to see that no one escapes the ritual.

The member who wears the mask to impersonate the doorkeeper is supposed to know the members of the society. You can pick out the members. They look scared. They look at you hard, or they pretend to be busy about some other business of their own. You can discern them through the mask. If any are reluctant to join, you have the power to force them, a strength against which they dare not resist. Sometimes fights occur. If one is not able, his partner, the other doorkeeper, will help him. Members *must* dance. Those who resist become possessed.

The round dance continues until certain songs request them to blow ashes. They repeat their square dance with the two matrons, blow ashes on their heads, receive tobacco, and depart. The feast is hulled-corn soup.

Although I have outlined the great public ritual, the same general pattern holds for private medicinal rites. The only difference is that the priest mentions the person's name in the tobacco invocation. Then the complexity of the ritual depends on the number of orders to which the patient belongs.

The simpler ceremony of the Common Faces alone has been vividly treated by Ernest Smith, a Seneca Indian artist of the Tonawanda reservation (pl. 25).

The Blowing Ashes Rite

The setting is the interior of a bark house, common among the Iroquois a few generations ago, and the time is presumably an evening of the Midwinter Festival. In response to a dream, the host has prepared a kettle of mush, or False-face pudding, and summoned the False-faces. The announcer, who is painted sitting on the bench, has returned thanks to all the Spirit-forces, explained the purpose of the feast, and invoked the Faces-of-the-forests with burning tobacco. They have entered. The singer straddles the bench to beat out the tempo for their dance, which they energetically commence, scattering ashes everywhere. They hasten to finish curing the patient, their host who stands before the fire, since they crave tobacco and hunger for the kettle of mush which he has set down for them. A tall, red-faced fellow vigorously rubs the patient's scalp before blowing the hot ashes into the seat of the pain. A dark one moans anxiously while rubbing hot ashes between his palms prior to pouncing on his victim's shoulder and pumping his arm. Across the fire, a red face stoops to scoop live coals, while another impatiently shakes a turtle rattle. They are naked above the waist, but wearing the masks is said to protect their bodies from cold and their hands from the burning embers.

Although the real Faces are seldom seen now, modern Iroquois, especially little children, fear them. A being which has the power to control disease, who can also cause the same ailment which he cures, is a subject for concern. The degree to which the False-faces dominate the lives of the Iroquois is well illustrated in the testimony of a sophisticated woman of Shawnee and Cayuga parentage whom Dr. Margaret Mead met among the Omaha. The informant had long since removed from her own tribesmen, but her childhood impression remained.

> I remember how scared I was of the False-faces; I didn't know what they were. They are to scare away disease. They used to come into the house and up the stairs and I used to hide away under the covers. They even crawled under the bed and they made that awful sound. When I was bad my mother used to say the False-faces would get me. Once, I must have been only 4 or 5, because I was very little when I left Canada, but I remember it so well that when I think of it I can hear that cry now, and I was going along a road from my grandfather's; it was a straight road and I couldn't lose my way, but it was almost dark, and I had to pass through some timber and I heard that cry and that rattle. I ran like a flash of lightning and I can hear it yet.

APPENDIX 5

REPORT ON THE BUREAU OF AMERICAN ETHNOLOGY

SIR: I have the honor to submit the following report on the field researches, office work, and other operations of the Bureau of American Ethnology during the fiscal year ended June 30, 1940, conducted in accordance with the act of Congress of March 16, 1939, which provides "* * * for continuing ethnological researches among the American Indians and the natives of Hawaii and the excavation and preservation of archeologic remains. * * *"

* * * *

Early in July 1939 Dr. William N. Fenton, associate anthropologist, left for Salamanca, N. Y., to conduct ethnobotanical studies among the Iroquois Indians of New York and Canada. He visited the Senecas of Allegany and Cornplanter Reservations, in southwestern New York and Pennsylvania, and the Mohawks of St. Regis Reservation, N. Y., and Caughnawaga, Province of Quebec. He called briefly on the Hurons of Lorette and the Mohawks of Oka, Lake of the Two Mountains, near Montreal. At Ottawa he studied the extensive catalog of Iroquois ethnological photographs in the National Museum of Canada. The month of August was passed among the Iroquois of Six Nations Reserve in Ontario, where he worked with Simeon Gibson, interpreter to the late J. N. B. Hewitt. About a hundred herbarium specimens were collected; when identified at the National Hebarium, these proved to be largely duplicates of medical plants gathered in previous years of field work among the Senecas. Moreover, interesting similarities of plant use and terminology were noted among Seneca, Mohawk, and Cayuga-Onondaga remnants who now live on widely separated reservations. Such resemblances suggest older basic Iroquois botanical concepts and medical practices. Photographs illustrating various activities in Iroquois herbalism comprise part of 100 negatives that were taken in the field. The early notes of F. W. Waugh were reviewed with Mohawk and Cayuga informants, and some paradigms in the several Iroquois dialects were recorded for comparative purposes. Returning to Allegany for the Green Corn Festival, Dr. Fenton reached Washington in mid-September.

During the winter's office work, Dr. Fenton read in the historical literature and located towns of the several Iroquois bands at successive periods in their history, with a view to outlining the major cultural problems arising from Iroquois tribal movements and conquests. This study, now published, attempts to begin for the Northeast the type of systematic approach that Dr. Swanton has accomplished for the Southeast. Dr. Fenton also published A Further Quest for Iroquois Medicines, in Explorations and Field-Work of the Smithsonian Institution in 1939, and An Herbarium from the Allegany Senecas, in The Historic Annals of Southwestern New York. Several lectures on various aspects of Iroquois culture were delivered to Washington audiences, and in June, Dr. Fenton addressed a regional meeting of botanists at the Allegany School of Natural History on Iroquois Ethnobotany.

On May 2, 1940, Dr. Fenton again left for Salamanca to resume field work among the Seneca. Working primarily at Allegany Reservation, he also visited Tonawanda, collecting early spring medicinal plants. This season, work with informants was combined with a project to study Iroquois masks and ceremonial equipment in museums located near the Iroquois. At the close of the fiscal year, the extensive Converse collections in the New York State Museum (Albany) and Montgomery County Historical Society (Fort Johnson), and the Boyle and Chiefswood collections in the Royal Ontario Museum of Archaeology (Toronto) were measured and photographed. The pictures have proved to be useful in eliciting new material from informants and promise future usefulness in establishing local types of carving. A complete record of the mask-making technique has been made together with photographs of crucial stages in the process, and the rituals of several shamanistic societies have been taken with a flash camera for the first time. Dr. Fenton was engaged in field work at the close of the fiscal year.

* * * *

Miss Densmore presented to the Bureau the original manuscript of an Onondaga Thanksgiving Song, written down for her in 1903 at Syracuse, N. Y., by Albert Cusick, a prominent Onondaga from the reservation near that city. The native words with their translation were also obtained. The song is in two parts, the lower being rhythmic and resembling a vocal accompaniment to the melody.

1. The Longhouse of Handsome Lake's followers in Onondaga Valley near Syracuse.

2. The Longhouse of the Onondagas of Six Nations on Grand River in Southern Ontario, Canada.

LONGHOUSES.

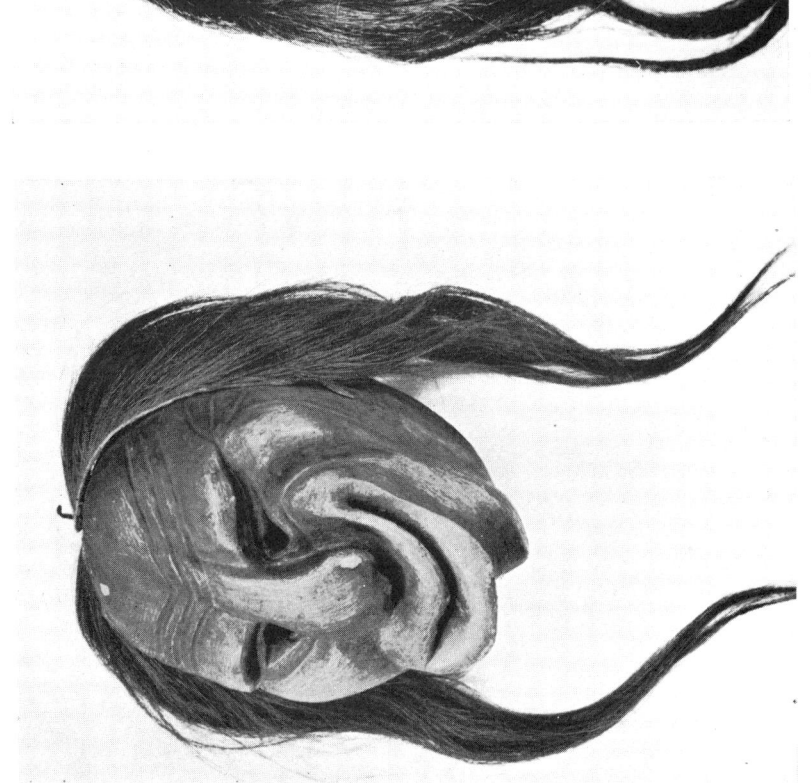

1. Carved by Elijah Hill, of Onandaga Reservation, N.Y. Museum of the American Indian, Heye Foundation, Cat. No. 8775.

2. Black wry-mouth mask characteristic of Iroquois of Grand River. New York State Museum, Cat. No. 37019.

CROOKED-MOUTH MASKS FROM THE ONONDAGA OF NEW YORK AND GRAND RIVER.

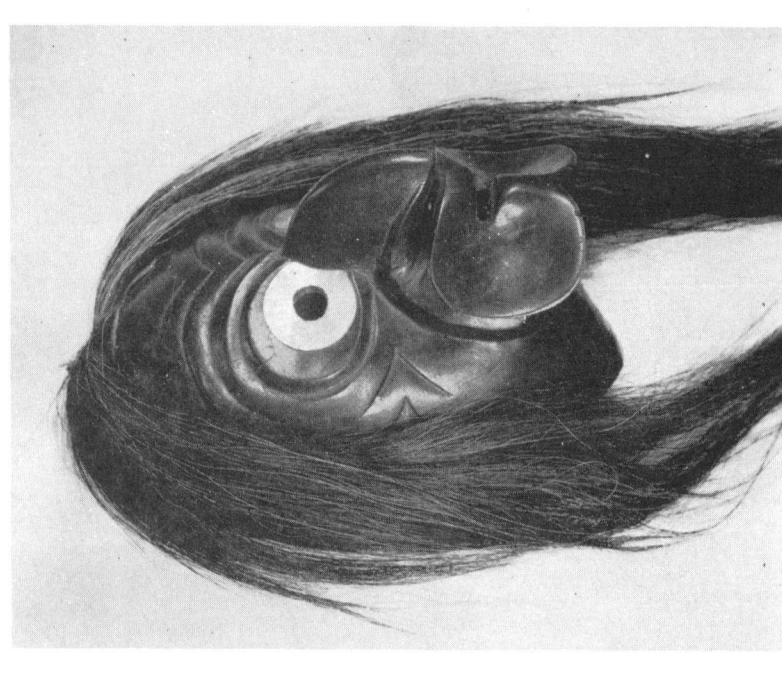

1. Black mask with red lips and spines on forehead. New York State Museum, Cat. No. 37023.
2. Red mask with gray hair. Rochester Museum of Arts and Sciences, Cat. No. AE 7.1.0/404.

STRAIGHT-LIPPED AND SPOON-LIPPED DOORKEEPER MASKS FROM THE SENECAS OF NEWTOWN, CATTARAUGUS RESERVATION, N. Y.

Smithsonian Report, 1940.—Fenton

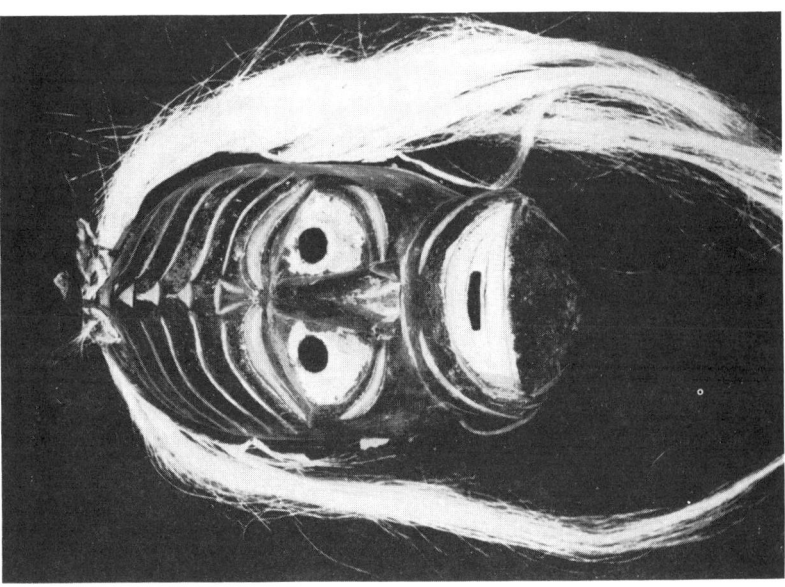

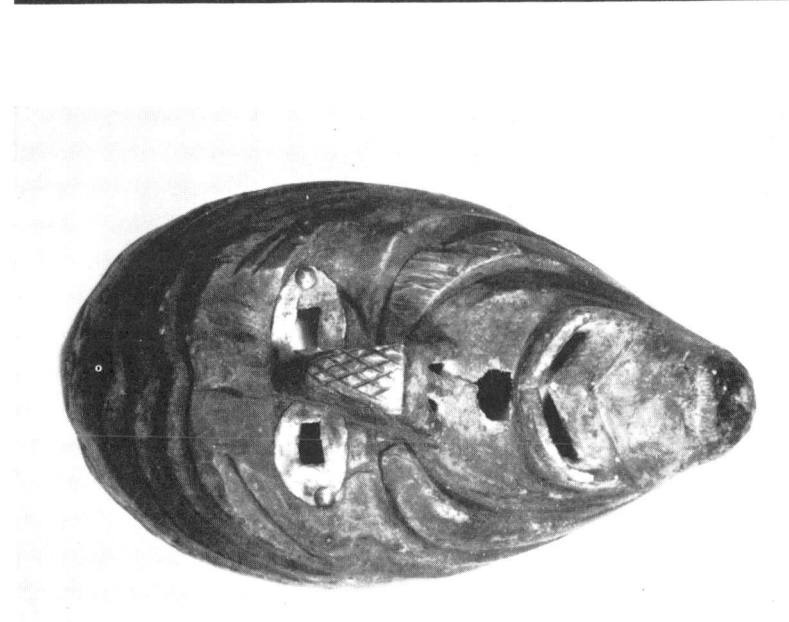

1. An early mask that traveled to Canada ca. 1775. New York State Museum, Cat. No. 37057.

2. An old red doorkeeper mask with white hair. New York State Museum, Cat. No. 37033.

THE HANGING MOUTH, LIKE THE MUSE OF TRAGEDY, IS AN OLD MASK TYPE WITH THE IROQUOIS.

1. Photograph from American Museum of Natural History, New York. Cat. No. 50/7214.
2. Photograph from American Museum of Natural History, New York. Cat. No. 50/7212.

MASKS WITH PROTRUDING TONGUES COLLECTED BY DECOST SMITH AT ONONDAGA CASTLE, N. Y., 1888.

Smithsonian Report, 1940.—Fenton PLATE 6

1. Made at Grand River about 1829 by John Styres and collected by David Boyle, 1899. Royal Ontario Museum of Archaeology, Cat. No. 17020.

2. The first Iroquois mask collected by an ethnologist, L. H. Morgan. Onondaga of Grand River, ca. 1850. New York State Museum, Cat. No. 36909.

HEAVY CARVING AND A LOLLING TONGUE ARE COMMON FEATURES IN MASKS FROM THE ONONDAGA OF GRAND RIVER.

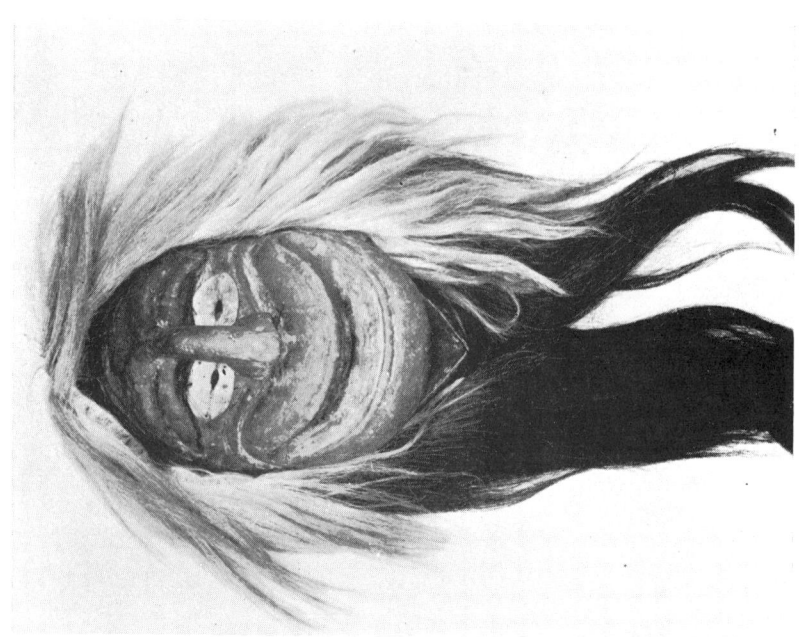

1. A smiling black beggar mask by Joanas Snow, a Seneca of Coldspring. Museum of the American Indian, Heye Foundation, New York, Cat. No. 20/2839.

2. A heavy mask with thick, smiling lips, from Grand River. Museum of the American Indian, Heye Foundation, New York, Cat. No. 1/2535.

NOT ALL THE MASKS ARE WRY-FACED; SOME ARE SMILING.

Smithsonian Report, 1940.—Fenton PLATE 8

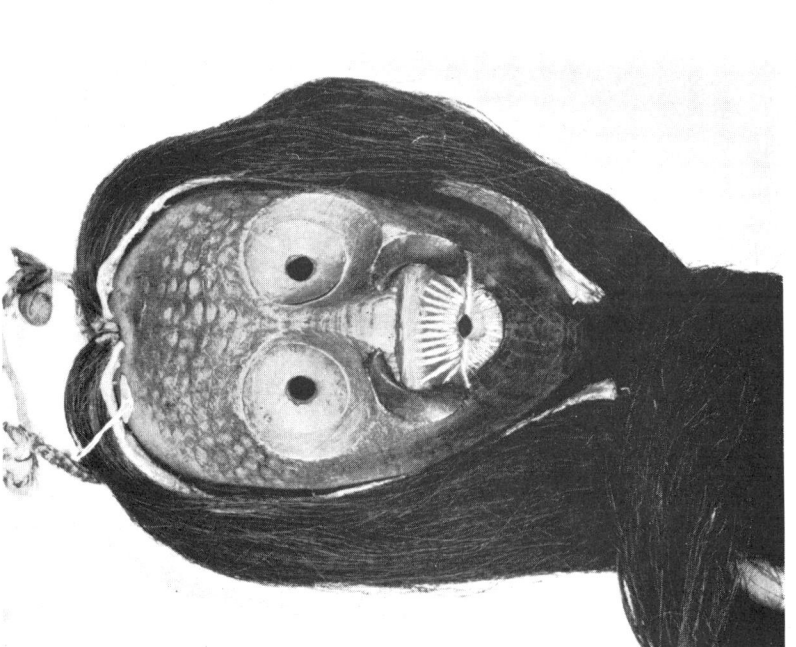

1. Red-faced whistler from Tonawanda (?) has a pock-marked forehead and long black hair. New York State Museum, Cat. No. 36867.

2. A black mask from Grand River; probably a likeness of the Whistling God. Royal Ontario Museum of Archaeology, Cat. No. HD 12634.

THE WHISTLING MASKS ARE LIKENESSES OF FOREST SPIRITS WHO MERELY WANT TOBACCO.

PLATE 9

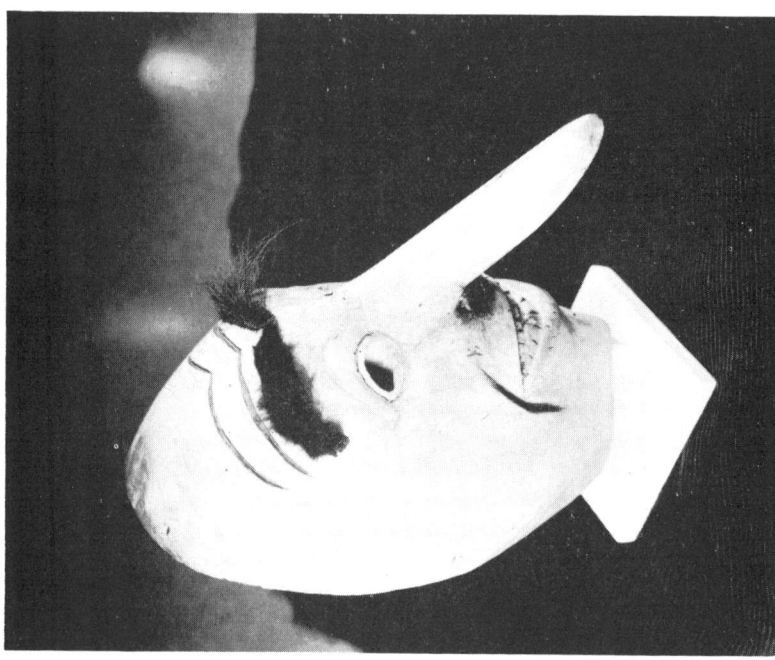

1. HE WHOSE BODY IS RIVEN IN TWAIN.

Divided mask, black and red, in typical Grand River style, by Jake Hess, Cayuga. Royal Ontario Museum of Archaeology.

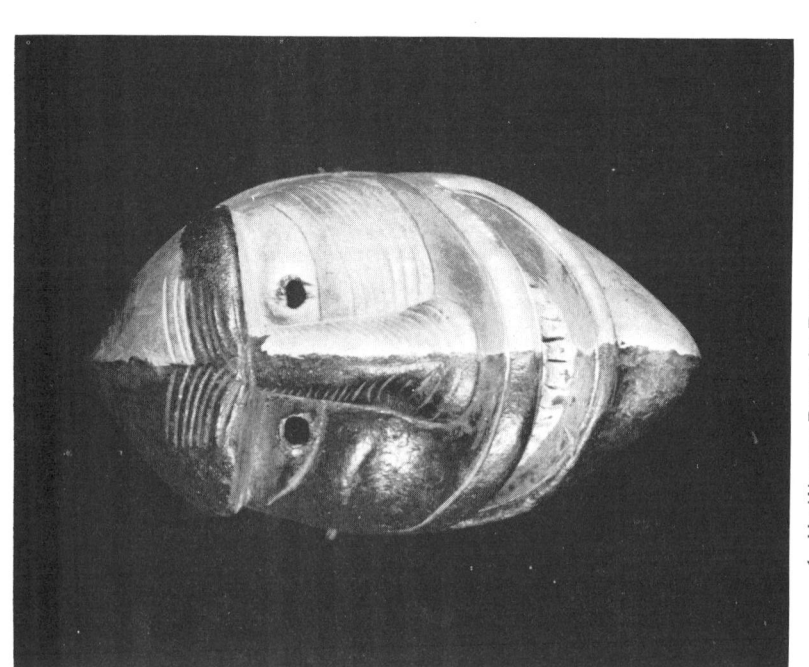

2. A LONG-NOSED MASK IMPROVISED FROM A PINE TRUNK AND BRANCH.

From the Cattaraugus Seneca. Museum of the American Indian, Heye Foundation, Cat. No. 20/1879.

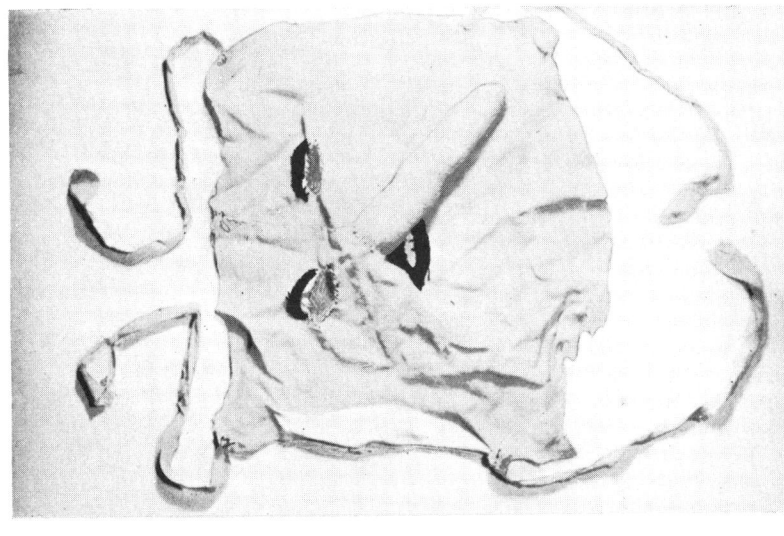

1. A puckish mask by Eli Schenandoah, Onondaga Reservation, N. Y. Collected by M. R. Harrington. Museum of the American Indian, Heye Foundation, Cat. No. 10975.

2. A cloth mask of Longnose made to frighten a naughty child, by Clara Redeye, Seneca, Allegany Reservation. U. S. National Museum.

LONGNOSE MASKS ARE CONSIDERED FUNNY.

1. So-called "buffalo" mask of Seneca. Note ears and earrings, present on some masks. New York State Museum, Cat. No. 37608.

2. Pig mask from Seneca of Cattaraugus. Buffalo Historical Society, Cat. No. 282.

ANIMAL MASKS ARE UNCOMMON AMONG THE IROQUOIS.

I'DOS SOCIETY MASK FROM SENECA OF GRAND RIVER RESERVE, ONTARIO, CANADA.
Museum of the American Indian, Heye Foundation, Cat. No. 6/1105.

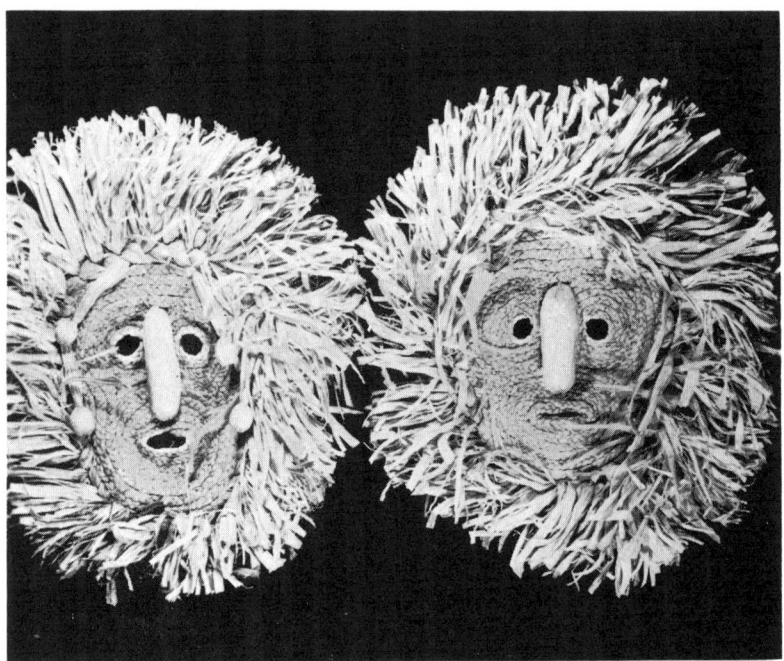

1. Grandmother and grandfather Bushy-head from Cattaraugus Senecas. Royal Ontario Museum of Archaeology, Cat. Nos. HD 8125 and 8126.

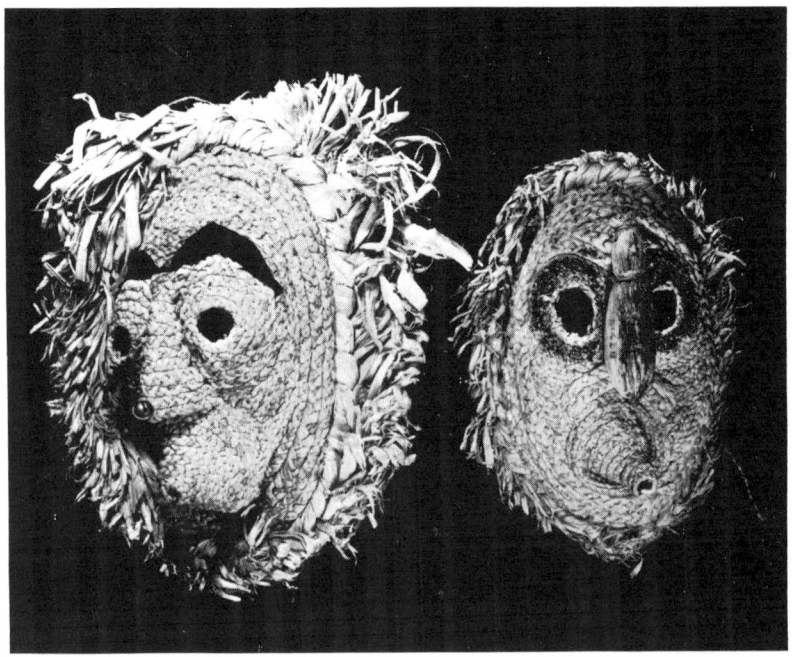

2. The rougher looking ones are old men; usually they have small, round mouths. Laidlaw Collection from Grand River, Royal Ontario Museum of Archaeology, Cat. Nos. 43347 and 21468.

HUSK FACES OR "BUSHY-HEADS" RESEMBLE BRAIDED FOOT MATS.

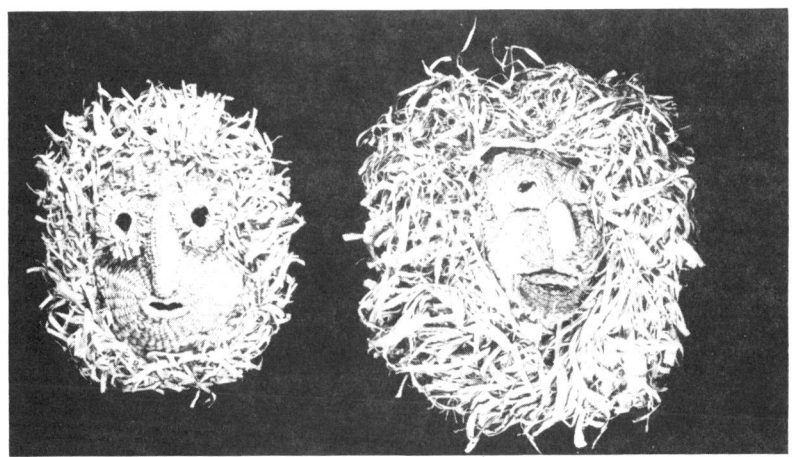

1. Left, twining commences at the mouth or nose; right, a braided bushy-head with puffy cheeks and red mouth. Senecas of Cattaraugus. New York State Museum, Cat. Nos. 36924 and 36922.

2. Iroquois husk face from Grand River, Canada. American Museum of Natural History, New York Cat. No. 110901.

TWINED HUSK FACES ARE NOW NEARLY OBSOLETE.

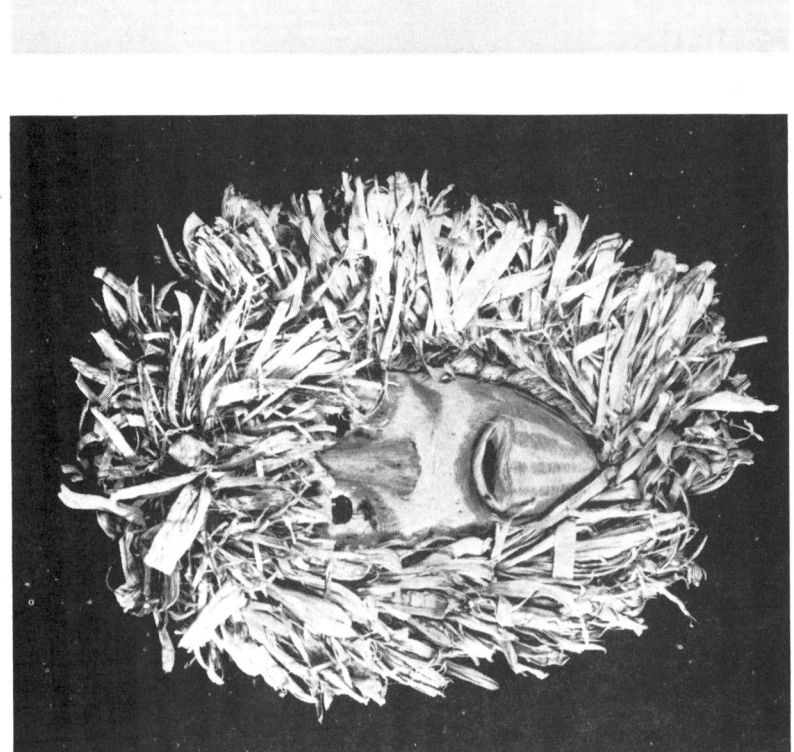

PLATE 15

1. The wooden bushy-head from the Onondaga of Six Nations, Grand River, Canada. New York State Museum, Cat. No. 37018.

2. Miniature personal guardian masks in characteristic art styles. Top, blind masquette from Grand River, with tobacco bag; left and right, spoon-lipped miniatures from Cattaraugus; bottom, Seneca miniature bushy-head. Museum of the American Indian, Heye Foundation, Cat. Nos. 2/4337, 6/1108, 2/9809, 7/9888.

STONE PIPE WITH BLOWING OR WHISTLING SPIRIT MASK FACING THE SMOKER, HAVING EXTENDED NARES, SUPPLEMENTARY WRINKLES AROUND MOUTH AND EYES OF IROQUOIS MASK STYLE.

Side view shows ears, sometimes present on masks, and in rear view one sees head ties or hair braids. Found below Sugar Run, emptying into Allegheny River above Warren, Pa. Courtesy of S. Farver, Palmyra, Pa.

PLATE 17

1. Our mighty protector traverses the earth. An Allegheny Seneca employs a blanket as a headthrow, dons his mask, and carries a turtle rattle to impersonate Shagodyowêhgo'wa', whose heavy tread shakes the earth.

2. Common Faces of the forests are cripples. Masks of the doorkeeper type frequently appear together with the Common Faces, and since the ritual prescribes a crawling posture for Common Faces and erect stature for doorkeepers, the bearing and gestures of the actor are more important than the type of mask he wears.

PLATE 18

1. THE BEGGARS AT THE MIDWINTER FESTIVAL AT TONAWANDA ARE A MOTLEY GROUP OF BOYS WHO SOMETIMES "TAKE SICK" AND JOIN THE SOCIETY.

2. AT COLDSPRING AMONG THE SENECAS A BLACK MASK IS SELECTED TO DANCE IN THE SOCIETY OF MYSTIC ANIMALS (HADI·"'DO'S) CEREMONY.

1. The Faces enter crawling.

2. Tobacco-burning invocation at the fire.

THE ORDER OF COMMON FACES WHO ENTER A HOUSE AND CURE.

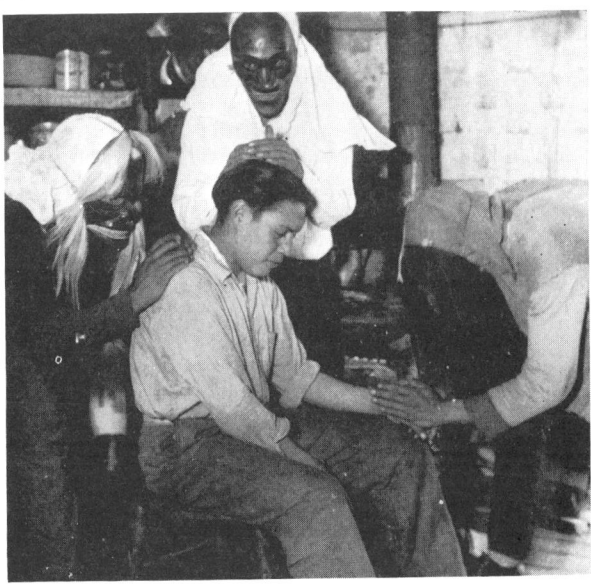

1. They cure by blowing hot ashes.

2. The ritual conductor pays their leader tobacco and they depart.

THE ORDER OF COMMON FACES WHO ENTER A HOUSE AND CURE.

1. THE FACE CARVED ON THE LIVING BASSWOOD TREE.
Courtesy of the Museum of the American Indian, Heye Foundation, New York.

2. THE OWNER SUPPLICATES HIS MASK WITH TOBACCO OFFERINGS WHEN IT FALLS, WHENEVER HE DREAMS OF IT, AND WHEN HE LOANS OR SELLS IT.

1. Hollowing out the inside of the mask with a bent farrier's knife.

2. Cutting the teeth and mouth detail.

CHAUNCEY JOHNNY JOHN MAKING A MASK.

PLATE 23

2. CHAUNCEY JOHNNY JOHN MAKING A BARK RATTLE.

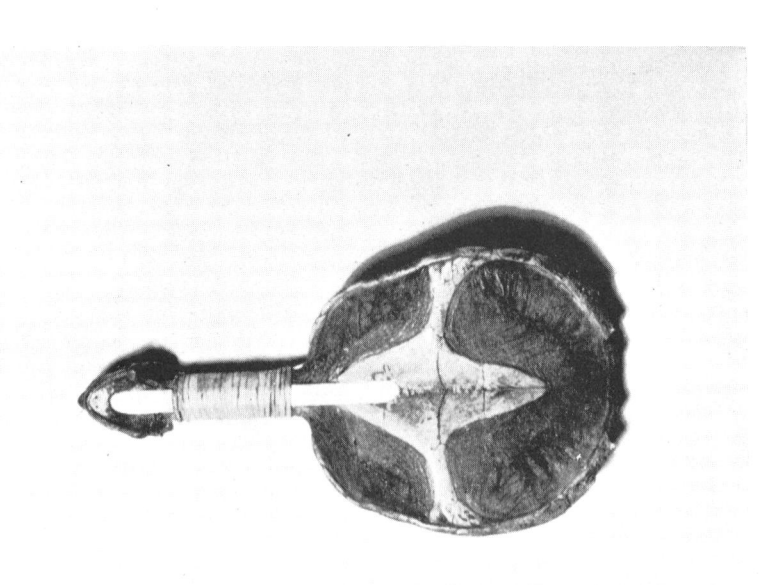

1. SNAPPING-TURTLE RATTLE. PEABODY MUSEUM, YALE UNIVERSITY.

Smithsonian Report, 1940.—Fenton PLATE 24

THE DOORKEEPER.

Shagodyowéhgo·wa· permits no one to enter or leave during his ritual. The mask, from Cattaraugus Reservation, is the property of the Rochester Museum of Arts and Sciences.

THE CURING RITE OF THE COMMON FALSE FACES.

Painting by Ernest Smith, Seneca Indian artist of the Tonawanda Reservation.

THE FALSE FACES IN STONE
Contemporary Iroquois Steatite Carvings from Ohsweken, Six Nations Reserve

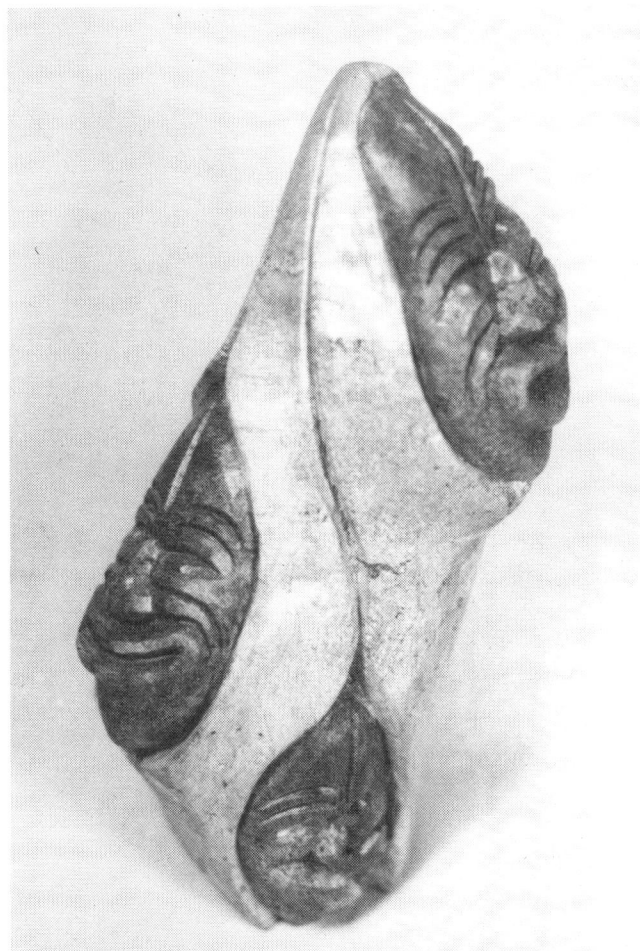

this page: **GROUP OF FACES**
by Ōdahaᵋ'dēts ("Not Good Enough"), Cayuga, Wolf clan.
Golden brown stone. Height 22.8 cm, maximum width 12 cm.
Registration number: 134-SN-2666-68.

overleaf: **FALSE FACE ON WORLD TURTLE**
by Sagōᵋwis ("He Strikes It"), Onondaga, Wolf clan.
Golden brown stone. Height 12.6 cm, width 14.8 cm.
Registration number: 53-SN-2905-14.

THE FALSE FACE BEING WITH TURTLE RATTLE ON WORLD TURTLE.
by Honnya'dēhō ("Crooked Sky"), Onondaga, Wolf clan.
Dark brown stone. Height 17 cm, width 18.7 cm.
Registration number: 104-SN-3330.

The small bodyless Face to the right is suggestive of the host of such Faces inhabiting the Forest and which occasionally reveal themselves to people.

photos by W. G. Spittal, Feb. 1984

A SIX NATIONS INDIAN CHIEF and HIS RELICS

JEREMIAH AARON (Sadāgan´hās – "Trees of Equal Height") a.k.a. "Jerry Blue-Eyes" c. 1930-1940. Aaron, a Faith-Keeper at Sour Springs Longhouse, posed for this picture (later made into a post card) while waiting for the anthropologist F G Speck. Among the eclectic mix of his display are: *left* – a tripod supports two box-lacrosse sticks, three rifles (one a percussion-cap), a pipe-tomahawk; *right* – an effigy pig on rockers keeps watch by Aaron's left leg; *center* – two ball-headed war clubs with metal blades in back of the balls are stuck into a block of wood; *background* – three turtle rattles, two of them the large size more suitable for carrying by False Faces than for accompanying a singer; a bow with quiver of arrows; two Corn Husk masks, each with pouches hanging from below the eyes and mouth, one has fringed husk "side-burns", the other a husk "goatee"; one of the four wood False Faces has a fur tail goatee. The unique "Smallpox and Measels" mask at far right was subsequently acquired by Speck and appears in plate IV of his *Midwinter Rites of the Cayuga Longhouse*.

WGS Collection

IROQRAFTS Indian Reprint Series

IROQRAFTS
Catalogue
Number   Title   ISBN-0-919645-

24-00300   **Scalping and Torture: Warfare Practices**   -10-0
             Among North American Indians
               Frederici, Nadeau, Knowles

24-00301   **Hair Pipes in Plains Indian Adornment**   -11-9
               J.C. Ewers

24-00302   **Indians of Ontario**   (Pending)   -12-7
               J.L. Morris

24-00303   **Wildwood Wisdom**   (Out of print)   -14-3
               E. Jaeger

24-00304   **Indian Uses of Wild Plants**   -16-X
               F. Densmore